Praise for *The Star of 2000*

Just as the angels once surprised the shepherds with amazing news, so *The Star of 2000* will delight readers everywhere with good news of great joy about Jesus and A.D. 2000.

—Dr. Bill Bright
President, Campus Crusade for Christ

What an important book. My perspective of the new millennium has just been profoundly shifted. My purpose now is to celebrate the birthday of Jesus. I wish everyone would read this book.

—Steve Vannoy
Author, *The 10 Greatest Gifts I Give My Children*

Jay Gary has written an in–depth look at this upcoming, unprecedented time in history, A.D. 2000. He calls forth the "jubilee generation" to be liberated from all the violence, emotional bondage and darkness of the heart, which is endemic to our age. He offers hope that the "odometer of history" will be reset to "zero." This is a prophetic call to hope amidst the travails of end times!!

—Joseph Paul Ozawa, Ph.D.
Psychologist and Pastor

The Star of 2000 is a wonderfully engaging b~ become so wrapped up with "winning our ~ lose the wonder of the person, Jesus

President, Evangelical Fellow.

The Star of 2000 describes a uniqu ....ty that the church of Jesus Christ has—the end of o. ...llennium and the start of another on 1 January 2001. Keep it on your desk . . . [and] refer to it regularly.

—Dr. David B. Barrett
Editor, *World Christian Encyclopedia*

Not since the publication of *Megatrends 2000* has a book grasped the awesome potential of the year 2000. Jay Gary has a global vision which surpasses denominational, racial and national barriers. He can already hear the music of the approaching Jubilee. He sees a new star of Bethlehem. His book will expand your vision and bring you hope. It is a book for all those who believe the best days of the church are still ahead!
—Dr. Joe A. Harding
Vision 2000, United Methodist Church

Jay Gary's unique and insightful book, *The Star of 2000*, is a dynamic wake-up call to history's greatest celebration ever—the 2,000th anniversary of Christ's birth. Jay Gary helps us dream of what this celebration could mean to honor and exalt Christ during this bimillennial if we'll just seize the moment to unwrap history's greatest treasure—the Lord Jesus Christ, Himself.
—Dick Eastman
International President, Every Home for Christ

One of the rarest commodities in today's world is genuine hope . . . This book makes me want to celebrate!
—John Dawson
Urban Ministries, Youth With a Mission

Some are called to carry out good strategy, others to lead them in doing so. A few, however, are actually called to be forerunners, pioneering the seed-thoughts which spawn tomorrow's strategies. Jay Gary, in his timely book, *The Star of 2000*, has opened an entirely new frontier of thought and activity for the church of the '90s.

Unique. Enlightening. Scholarly. Inspirational. Interesting. Rarely can all of these words be used to describe one book, but here it is. As you read it you'll agree with Jay, "Let the celebration begin!"
—Dutch Sheets
Senior Pastor, Springs Harvest Fellowship

There is a sign over my desk that reads, "Come Holy Spirit, pour down upon us a gift of creative genius for the Year 2000." In *The Star of 2000*, Jay Gary shows this gift in a variety of ways. Among the many creative ideas he shares are "25 ways to light a candle for Christ by the year 2000." If you are looking for inspiration and challenge in anticipation of the year 2000, here is a book well worth reading, and *praying over* as well.

—**Fr. Tom Forrest, C.Ss.R.**
Evangelization 2000

The Star of 2000 is not only well researched and written, but it tugs at the emotions and heartstrings of hope for all people. With a ring of objectivity, yet combined with a realization of the divinity of Jesus, life is truly manifested in the chapters. Glory to God in the highest! May the year 2000 truly be the benchmark for all humanity!

—**Bob Garner**
Film/Television Producer

Jay Gary has discovered and effectively documented the quintessence of the bimillennium—the universal invitation to celebrate the person and impact of Jesus Christ! In a very readable style, this volume provides a biblical and historical perspective of the significance of A.D. 2000. Enthusiasm and hope will spring up in those who read this book! I heartily recommend it to every Christian and world leader.

—**Jim Hodges**
Senior Elder, Church of the King

Our Lord is giving His church special opportunities for ministry as this decade draws to conclusion and a new millennium is about to begin. Every committed Christian could benefit from prayerfully considering the significant insights shared by Jay Gary in this "thought-provoking" volume.

—**Dr. Paul Cedar**
President, The Evangelical Free Church of America

This is an incredibly prophetic book. Jay Gary has peered into the spirit realm and drawn from God's secret place. He declares that the church must prepare a celebration, a festival for, about and with Jesus, our honored guest and royal Bridegroom. *The Star of 2000* is infused with biblical revelation of fullness, sonship, maturity, and perfection of the glorious triumphant church—the Feast of Tabernacles. Read the book.
—Clarice Fluitt
Pastor, Eagle's Nest Church

The Star of 2000 can set a powerful agenda for pastors, churches, missions and the media. This positive message of the all glorious Jesus supersedes the doom and gloom prognosticators of this decade.
—Gary Clark
Holy Spirit Renewal Ministries, American Baptist Churches

A global celebration of unparalleled magnitude is about to begin. *The Star of 2000* is an invitation and challenge to lift this occasion to its loftiest height in honor of the only one worthy of this tribute, Jesus! Jay Gary masterfully offers the meaning and importance of A.D. 2000 to your family, church and city. Don't miss this unique book!
—Mr. Paul Eshleman
The *JESUS* Project

Do you need a fresh infusion of hope in your life? Jay Gary provides it in vast quantities in *The Star of 2000*. Even more, he stimulates many creative options for putting that hope to work for you . . . and for Christ. Your heart will sing!
—David Bryant
President, Concerts of Prayer International

The STAR of 2000

Our Journey Toward Hope

JAY GARY

Bp

Bimillennial Press
Colorado Springs, Colorado

Copyright © 1994 by Jay E. Gary
All rights reserved.

No part of this book may be reproduced in any form or by any electronic or mechanical means, including photocopying, recording, or any information storage and retrieval systems, without prior permission in writing from the publisher, except by a reviewer, who may quote brief passages in a review. All inquiries should be addressed to Bimillennial Press, P.O. Box 1777, Colorado Springs, Colorado 80901-1777.

Scripture used in this work, unless otherwise indicated, is taken from the HOLY BIBLE: NEW INTERNATIONAL VERSION © 1973, 1978, 1984 by International Bible Society. Used by permission of Zondervan Bible Publishers.

Printed in the United States of America

Printing number
99 98 97 96 95 94   5 4 3 2 1

Book cover design: Bradley Lind

Library of Congress Cataloging-in-Publication Data

Gary, Jay, 1954–
    The star of 2000: our journey toward hope / by Jay Gary

        p.   cm.
    Includes bibliographical references (p. 165-166) and index.
    ISBN 0-9641388-0-8
    1. Jesus Christ—Anniversaries, etc.   2. Two thousand, A.D.
3. Jesus Christ—Significance.   I. Title.
BT590.A55G3 1994   94-21828
232—dc20   CIP

This book is available at special discounts in bulk purchases for promotions, premiums or educational use. For details contact: Special Sales Director, Bimillennial Press, P.O. Box 1777, Colorado Springs, CO 80901-1777.

This book is dedicated
to the Magi everywhere
who decide to join
this journey toward hope.

incarnati Verbi mysterium
lux tuae claritatis

Acknowledgements

It took the work of many people to make this book true to its ideal and true to what is real. I especially offer thanks:

For my wife and partner on the journey, Olgy, who first saw this book as *The Star of 2000*.

For believing in me and the dream: Maria Olga Aleu, Larry & Bernice Gary, Steve & Ruth Carter, Jack & Nell Chancey, Gene & Vivian Davis, George & Clarice Fluitt, Andy & Chantal Lakey, Tim & Elena Poulin, Andy & Gerri Robinson, Bob & Jan Stennett and Robin & Nancy Wainwright.

For those who lent me their ears and offered me pearls of wisdom: Steve Hawthorne and Steve Johnson.

For my editors: Jane Crane, Brenda Franklin and Tanya Price, who brought their impeccable taste to improve this manuscript and saved me from many inelegances and howlers.

For those who held me true to my own words: John Burglehaus, Dick Durant, Ron Symons and Rusty Wright, all of whom read the manuscript with care.

For those who offered their good name and precious time by writing endorsements.

Contents

CONTENTS

The STAR of 2000

Twinkle, twinkle, little star,
how I wonder what you are ...

A Magnet Hung in Time

Little children are fascinated by their power to attract and repel. As adults, we hardly give any thought to the magnets which surround us. Little do we realize how our lives have been shaped by a huge magnet hung in time: the year 2000.

Reaching far beyond human understanding, the attraction of the year 2000 has touched the popular imagination. We should almost expect something to happen in the cosmos, so that we might read this great date in the sky.

It's become commonplace to imagine how the change of the calendar from 1999 to 2000 and the advent of the third millennium in 2001 will galvanize attention around the world. Hundreds of products are now marketed with a year 2000 product label, and the media refers regularly to the anticipation of the biggest New Year's Eve in a thousand years.

What we have yet to see in reference to the turn of the millennium is Jesus, the Star of 2000. We have yet to realize that the civilization which began with His birth, some 2,000 years ago, will soon commemorate His bimillennial. He is the real attraction of the magnet year 2000.

15

Personally, I am in awe of Jesus of Nazareth. Everything about Him astounds me. The way He spoke, the way He healed, the way He came into this world and left it while still remaining—it all amazes me.

No one would let the 100th anniversary of their grandmother's birth go by without giving her a tremendous birthday celebration. In a similar way, we shouldn't let the 2,000th anniversary of the birth of Jesus pass by without giving Him a magnificent tribute. In His honor, the year 2000 ought to be the most significant celebration in the history of civilization.

The first half of this book looks at the significance of the year 2000 and asks, "Why should Jesus' bimillennial be celebrated?" In this section you will discover why Jesus is in a class all by Himself, and meet various "Magi" who have seen His star. You'll also learn how the anticipation of the most memorable Christmas ever will affect society well before A.D. 2000.

The second half of the book asks, "How could our cities celebrate Christ's 2,000th jubilee?" Chapters 8 to 11 look at some possibilities: extraordinary prayer, festivals of praise, public processions and intercultural celebrations. You will also find ideas on how Christ might be honored in your life, family, and community as you look to A.D. 2000.

If you would like to see Christ publicly honored during this bimillennial era of 1996–2001, this book is for you.

As you set your sight on the Star of 2000, may you be drawn past the party of 2000 to the person of Christ. Like the Magi, may you reach your destination on this historic journey in time to give Him your greatest gift.

Jay Gary
June 25, 1994
Colorado Springs

*We saw his star in the east
and have come to worship him.*
—Matthew 2:2

PROLOGUE

A Parable of the Fourth Wise Man

You ask me who I am! That is simple. I am Zalshar, the fourth wise man who saw the star of Bethlehem. What is that you ask!

Yes, most people think there were only three Magi, Melchoir, Gaspar and Balthasar.[1] They saw the heavenly sign from Persia. But they were not the only ones to see the star of wonder.

I saw the great star too, from Arabia.[2] It appeared one night as I was gazing into the heavens. I knew the universe was about to bring forth a progeny, far beyond our understanding. Great hope filled my land, for the people expected the next prophet to appear in a foreign country. I set out on horseback to follow this moving star, and present my gifts to the newborn King.

Why haven't you heard of me! I am ashamed to say. All right, I'll tell you. I got lost along the way.

After I got my bearings , I finally made it to Jerusalem. It was there I expected to find the newborn King in glory. Yet through a dream I was told, "Not in glory, but in humility."

Later I learned the sacred writings foretold the King would be born in Bethlehem. By the time I arrived in this small town, I had missed the miracle of the first Christmas.

The Child was nowhere to be found, and left no trail. For months I searched the land, seeking to pay homage to the newborn King. After two years, I returned home from the land of Israel, a tired and bewildered man.

It was some 30 years later that I began to hear reports about a rabbi named Jesus. This one, so they said, was full of wisdom and understanding, counsel and power. Right away I felt this must be the one whom I had missed so long ago.

Yet the next report I received bore sad tidings. The life of this wise one was cut short, through death on a tree. The words came back to me, "Not in glory, but in humility."

Around this time I noticed that those I loved were growing older, while I aged not. My wife and brothers passed away, while I lived on. The years passed, and I watched my children age, while I stayed the same. Why was this so?

Was I here to search for the true spirit of Christmas until I found it? Would I follow that Star, wherever it led, until the whole world saw Him?

In the second century, I was full of joy when the bishop of Rome urged his people to sing "in celebration of the birthday of our Lord." People were singing Christmas hymns across the Roman Empire, stretching from Britain to India.

In A.D. 315, I learned of a kindhearted bishop who was honoring children with gifts as I once sought to do for the Christ Child. I traveled to the city of Myra, on the coast of Asia Minor.

I met Bishop Nicholas during one of his rounds. He truly was a godly and generous man, worthy to be later named St. Nicholas, the patron saint of children. Perhaps you know him as Santa Claus.

By A.D. 354, people finally began to celebrate the "feast of the Nativity" on December 25th. The spirit of giving began to burn brighter.

Many centuries passed with Christmas being observed as a religious festival. I wondered if the world would ever see the Star again.

Then along came St. Francis of Assisi. Here was one who understood the true meaning of Christmas.

I was there in A.D. 1223, when St. Francis placed a crib and live animals in the chapel at Grecchio, Italy. Upon seeing this on Christmas Eve, the children exclaimed in awe and admiration, "It's like the stable of Bethlehem!" Tears filled my eyes as I gazed on this nativity scene, as I remembered how I had missed the first one in Bethlehem.

Soon the people began holding nativity plays to act out the mystery of the incarnation. After the drama, I would join the people on their way home as they sang Christmas carols.

I said to myself, "Finally the world is beginning to learn the true spirit of Jesus, 'not in glory, but in humility.'"

The centuries passed, and others arose to illuminate the divine mystery. Whether through Handel's Messiah, *or Charles Dickens' Christmas books, people kept the true spirit of Christmas alive.*

Yet I kept waiting for the time when the whole world would find the Prince of Peace.

Now as the year 2000 approaches, Christmas is observed widely as a holiday and less as a holy day. Modern man has lost the original passion, which filled us on our first journey as Magi.

Will I find the true spirit of giving again as the world prepares for the 2,000th anniversary of the birth of Jesus? There is talk in the land that a new advent will come in time for the new millennium.

My nights are spent much like I did 2,000 years ago, in prayer, gazing into the heavens. That feeling is back. Like in the days of old, my eyes are fixed on the horizon, waiting for the Star I once saw to appear again.[3]

If this ancient desire wells up in your heart, as it has in mine, get ready for a wonderful journey. Another spiritual procession will certainly begin before the year 2000. This time we must not lose our bearings.

Perhaps we shall meet along the way in time to celebrate the bimillennial by giving Him our greatest gift.

*The year 2000 is the most far-reaching
initiative in human history.*
—*Don Toppin*

1

The Bimillennial Era
Has Begun

Bob Jani should have been called Mr. Celebration. This man
was known as Disney's "builder of spectaculars." He created
the Main Street Electrical Parade. His pageantry opened Disney
World and Epcot Center. In the mid-'70s, he reopened Radio
City Music Hall and choreographed the bicentennial celebrations for New York—complete with tall ships and fireworks.
He orchestrated Reagan's second inaugural, and designed the
opening ceremonies for the 1984 Olympics in Los Angeles.

All along, however, Bob Jani had a secret dream—to prepare
the world for the 2,000th anniversary of the birth of Jesus.

For more than ten years he traveled to the world's great
museums to collect slides of art work on Jesus. He reasoned,
"if a picture is worth a thousand words, then the art work of
Jesus could tell His story better than all the literature in the
world put together." By the late '80s he had collected over
50,000 slides of Christ for his image base.

But tragedy struck in 1989. At the age of 55, Bob Jani died
an untimely death due to Lou Gehrig's disease.

When I heard this, I asked the Lord, "Why?" Then I

remembered Jesus' words, "I tell you the truth, unless a kernel of wheat falls to the ground and dies, it remains only a single seed. But if it dies, it produces many seeds" (John 12:24).

As you will see in these chapters, Bob Jani's work is alive and well today. His dream to celebrate the 2,000th birthday of our Lord is spreading to the hearts of millions.

A Magnificent Celebration

The time has come for the world to make the year 2000 what it is truly meant to be—the greatest celebration in the history of civilization—in honor of the 2,000th anniversary of the birth of Jesus.

When Uncle Sam marked his 200th birthday in 1976, our communities rolled out an entire year of events, including sporting contests, history exhibits and art festivals, all to celebrate our nation's bicentennial.

In just a short time, our world will have the incredible opportunity to celebrate its bimillennial—the 2,000th birthday of its only Savior, Jesus Christ. He is worthy of the greatest celebration in the history of civilization.

No one has ever touched history like Jesus of Nazareth. People of practically every culture and background acknowledge Him as the greatest teacher, the greatest leader, the person who lived the most holy life. Indeed, there has never been anyone who could compare with Jesus Christ. He is unique among human beings. For 2,000 years His life has been an inspiration to poets, painters, musicians, philosophers, scientists, politicians and humanitarians. The arrival of the year 2000 will undoubtedly be marked by extensive secular celebrations. At the heart of these celebrations, however, should be a magnificent observance of Jesus' bimillennial.

A Wake Up Call From God!

In the fall of 1984, George Heiner was a second-year dental student in San Francisco, with little more than lab work on his mind. He had never given any thought to the year 2000, but that abruptly changed on the morning of October 9th.

"It must have been about 4 a.m. when I awoke from the most powerful dream of my life. I was in a room filled with angels singing praises," Heiner shares. "I got up quickly, sat at my desk, and wrote down these words: 'There is going to be a celebration in the year 2000 of song and praise celebrating faithfulness in Jesus Christ.'"

Within six months Heiner launched an organization which has begun to plan a celebration for the year 2000 through the arts, television, drama and music. Within a year, Heiner had distributed more than 200 licenses for use of his "Celebration 2000 A.D." logo to groups with year 2000 goals.

Consisting of an artistic rendition of the portrait of Jesus Christ inscribed on a coin, "the logo points to a celebration at the culmination of the 20th century." Heiner claims the logo is the heart of a communications strategy designed to link groups together in their mission efforts for the year 2000.

His most recent project under *Action Music* was "Mission 2000 A.D.," a music cassette with interviews by Pat Robertson, Bill Bright and other well-known religious leaders. On their full page magazine ad, printed in large letters, is the statement: "Listen to What's Uniting All of Christianity. Beyond Music & the Unbelievable. Mission 2000—It's Worldwide."

"The celebration I am involved in planning," claims Heiner, "is not limited to Christians by any means. We all have birthdays and those dates record our history in reference to the birth and life of Jesus Christ B.C./A.D."

The Journey of the Magi 2000

For more than a hundred years at Christmas time children have sung, "Star of wonder, star of night, star with royal beauty bright; Westward leading, still proceeding, guide us to thy perfect light." Now as we approach A.D. 2000, the spiritual journey of the wise men could be reenacted before our eyes.

Since 1991, Robin Wainwright, an entrepreneur who lives in Northern California, has been planning to commemorate the 2,000th anniversary of the journey of the Magi beginning in 1998.

It all started while reading the Christmas story to his three children. Robin came up with a novel idea. "Why don't we reenact the 2,000th anniversary of the journey of the Magi? I mean with horses and camels over the original Middle East route!"

"Right, Dad," said Mark, then 12 years old, who had experienced his father's reckless outdoor adventures.

Over the next year, however, Robin read everything he could find which speculated on the original overland route of the Magi. Upon showing his research and maps to his now teenage son, Mark agreed to go with him to the Middle East.

That first expedition took father and son to meet with government officials in the Middle East to ask for permission to retrace the overland journey of the wise men with horses and camels.

By 1994, a working committee had already been organized in the Middle East. Plans call for the opening of a "Journey of the Magi" visitor's center in Bethlehem, complete with a planetarium! In addition, Robin envisions consultations on human rights, and a host of cooperative projects from 1998 to 2001 by child and refugee agencies to commemorate the 2,000th anniversary of Jesus' flight into Egypt.

As we approach the bimillennial, this project could impact millions of young people, especially in the Middle East, where the blessings of the Prince of Peace are yet to be felt.

From Bicentennial to Bimillennial

I like to refer to A.D. 2000 as the "bimillennial," "bi" meaning two, together with "millennial"—a thousand, refers to a two-thousandth anniversary.

Just as the United States had a bicentennial in 1976 to

celebrate it's 200th anniversary, so the world will have a bimillennial in 2000 to mark the 2,000th anniversary of the birth of it's only Savior.

Preparations for celebrations began long before the American bicentennial in 1976. The United States officially opened its bicentennial era in 1971.

I feel it is not too early to say the bimillennial era of Jesus has begun. As with any centennial or bicentennial, a bimillennial would have a series of major themes and common programs, all associated through international years, weeks and days leading up to its culmination. We will likely see this era of commemoration of Christ develop from 1996 to 2001.

Bimillennial tributes to Jesus will fill our cities' churches, theaters, libraries, museums and stadiums. The Scriptures say we have been chosen for this very purpose, "that you may declare the praises of Him who called you out of darkness into His wonderful light" (1 Peter 2:9).

A Decade of Destiny

You might ask, "If the bimillennial era has begun, why haven't I heard about it until now?" My reply is that you probably have, but in different words. Up until now, we have thought of the bimillennial in terms of a "decade of destiny."

None of us will ever forget how the last half of 1989 opened a new epoch in world history. On June 4th, the morning after the Tiananmen Square massacre of students, television commentator Charles Kuralt summarized how we all felt, "This is a morning on which you can almost feel the world changing."

Even though the old guard in China refused to acknowledge the new day, hope spread like wildfire through Eastern Europe. First communism collapsed in Poland, then Germany, followed by Czechoslovakia, and finally Romania. By the end of 1989, the Berlin Wall was down, and we knew in our hearts that the Cold War era had ended. As we entered the 1990s many proclaimed it a "decade of destiny."

The Celebration of Centuries

What I am now seeing is that what began as a "decade of destiny" will climax in a "celebration of centuries."

During the late '80s, I worked for the Lausanne movement, founded by Billy Graham. As a conference planner for church leaders, I began to notice how the agenda began to pivot toward A.D. 2000.

Practically every major denomination dedicated the years 1990–2000 to world outreach. In addition, more than 100 mission groups set goals to reach the world for Christ.

Never before had it seemed that God said the same thing to so many leaders, from so many continents, about such a specific decade of evangelism. And all this leading up to A.D. 2000.

This "decade of harvest" impression was so strong that I eventually wrote *The Countdown Has Begun* to tell the story of how leaders were joining hands to fulfill the great commission by the year 2000.[1]

Only afterward did I realize I was so consumed with what we should *do* by A.D. 2000 and beyond, I almost missed the *who*.

By the end of 1990, I felt our Lord saying, "Don't forget to invite *Me* to the party!"

I began to wonder . . . is the world really asking for a massive "Target 2000" campaign where the church tries once more to rally its troops to fight the mother of all missionary battles?

Rather than a confrontation, perhaps the world is waiting for an invitation. Having first feasted at the banquet table of the living God, the church will in turn go out to invite others to come to Christ's celebration 2000.

I began to see A.D. 2000 in a new light, not just confined to its dramatic "decade of destiny" opening, but in terms of its consummation as a "celebration of centuries." It was time to get ready for Jesus' bimillennial.

Wise Men Still Seek Him

Everywhere I go these days, I find people hungry to know God. They may not have put words to it, but once they hear about the 2,000th anniversary of the birth of Jesus, their heart cries, "That's it! I want to follow that Star of wonder."

Today, the average follower of Jesus is overfed, over-programmed, and oversold. They have met Christ at some resting spot along their journey. Yet they only know Him from afar, despite all their efforts.

I believe the Spirit of God will use preparations for the bimillennial to call forth a genuine movement of seekers. Their hearts will tell them there is something more, and they will turn in spiritual procession once again to seek the fullness of Christ, "in whom are hidden all the treasures of wisdom and knowledge" (Colossians 2:3).

The whole world knows that a new millennium is about to begin. This awareness is so strong that *Time* magazine put out a special issue on the year 2000 in the fall of 1992.

Up until now, however, we may have only seen the year 2000 as the biggest New Year's Eve in a 1,000 years. Society in large has been unaware that the bimillennial era has quietly begun.

I believe soon we will see A.D. 2000 as the most meaningful Christmas in 2,000 years. When that starts to happen, the whole world will experience a new awakening in light of the new millennium.

*As the centuries pass the evidence is
accumulating that . . . Jesus is the most
influential life ever lived on this planet.
—Kenneth Scott Latourette*

2

Unwrap History's Mystery

According to historians, Virgil was the greatest Roman poet who ever lived. His *Aeneid* was almost a Roman bible.

It tells the story of a wandering hero, Aeneas, who after the fall of Troy, set out to found a new Troy, an eternal home for the gods and his companions. He almost forgets his mission along the way, but a spirit guides him to the lower world, where he is shown the great heroes, yet unborn, who were to make Rome great. On arriving at the Tiber, Aeneas defeats a rival to marry the daughter of King Latinus, the ancestor of the Romans.

Virgil's *Aeneid* became the national epic poem of Rome because it exalted the virtues of the Roman people. It also established that Rome ruled in accordance with a divine plan, a belief that was important to the birth of the *Pax Romana*, a peace that lasted 200 years.

In 1981, the Italian city of Mantua celebrated the 2,000th anniversary of the death of Virgil (70–19 B.C.). The Virgilian bimillennial went largely unnoticed outside of Italy.

Contrast this, if you will, with the coming bimillennial of

Jesus. The 2,000th anniversary of His birth will likely eclipse and overshadow the bimillennial of any other figure, becoming the greatest celebration in the history of civilization.

Jesus Is Unique

The clear question is, "Why? What is the difference between these two persons?" Both men were products of antiquity. Each inspired empires, one political, the other spiritual. Why would Jesus be honored the world over with a celebration of centuries, and Virgil just a celebration by one city?

The answer is obvious—Jesus is in a class all by Himself. He is unique. He stands alone. "Jesus was the greatest religious genius that ever lived," said Ernest Renan, the 19th century French historian. "His beauty is eternal, and his reign shall never end. Jesus is in every respect unique, and nothing can be compared with him."[1]

Christ's life is the point from which the majority of the world dates all of history, B.C. to A.D. It is impossible to understand world civilization without understanding the founder of Christianity. Indeed, all history is incomprehensible without Him!

Yale historian Jaroslav Pelikan opens his classic book *Jesus Through the Centuries* by writing, "Regardless of what anyone may personally think or believe about him, Jesus of Nazareth has been the dominant figure in the history of Western culture for almost twenty centuries." Pelikan then asks rhetorically, "If it were possible, with some sort of super magnet, to pull up out of that history every scrap of metal bearing at least a trace of his name, how much would be left?"[2]

A Man Without Equal

No one has ever touched history like Jesus. Dr. Bill Bright, founder of Campus Crusade for Christ, tells of an encounter with a brilliant young medical student from a foreign country, who was a devout follower of an eastern religion.

Dr. Bright asked this student several questions, "Who in your opinion is the greatest leader the world has ever known?" "Who has done the most good for mankind?" After a moment of hesitation, the student replied, "I am sure that Jesus has done more good than anyone who has ever lived. I would say that He is the greatest leader."

Then Dr. Bright asked, "Who do you think is the greatest teacher?" No doubt he considered Socrates, Aristotle, Plato, Confucius and the other great philosophers of ancient and modern times. But the young man answered, "The greatest teacher is Jesus."

Finally, Dr. Bright asked him, "In your opinion, who in the entire history of civilization has lived the most holy life?" Immediately, he answered, "There has never been anyone like Jesus."

Indeed, as Dr. Bright says, "there has never been anyone who could compare with Jesus of Nazareth. He is unique among all the human beings who have ever been born." He is truly worthy of our praise.[3]

The Legacy of Jesus

If one were to list the unique contributions Jesus left civilization they would certainly include:

- ◆ The fatherhood of God—we can intimately address God as "Abba" father.

- ◆ The kingdom of heaven—the age to come of God's reign has already begun and will soon replace the present order of world history.

- ◆ The family of nations—people from the East and West will one day live together in harmony.

- ◆ The law of love—true religion goes beyond outward observance to the renewal of one's spirit to fulfill the law of loving one another.

- The victory over death—God triumphs over misery, pain and evil, not through force, but through self-sacrifice on the cross.

- The hope of resurrection—our souls will be reunited with resurrected bodies in the age to come.

Whatever the future may bring, the contributions of Jesus will not be surpassed. Throughout the ages, people will proclaim that among the sons of men, there is none born who is greater than Jesus. Of His originality, George Gordon writes:

> . . . he is in the sphere of the spirit original in the profoundest sense; he is original in himself, in his power to revive dead wisdom, to stamp with his character the unvalued truth, and put it in everlasting social circulation; his is original in depth of insight, in purity of vision, in the transcendence of mind, the universality of his appeal. In Jesus we find, in the highest degree, originality of character.[4]

The Incomparable Christ

Surely there has been no greater vision of who we are and what we might become, whether personally or socially, than Jesus. If you had to give a tribute to Jesus, what would you say? Consider this essay:

> More than nineteen hundred years ago there was a man born contrary to the laws of life. This man lived in poverty and was reared in obscurity. He did not travel extensively. Only once did He cross the boundary of the country in which He lived; that was during His exile in childhood.

> He possessed neither wealth nor influence. His relatives were inconspicuous, and had neither training nor formal education. In infancy He startled a king; in childhood He puzzled doctors; in manhood He ruled the course of nature, walked upon the billows as if

pavements, and hushed the sea to sleep. He healed the multitudes without medicine and made no charge for His service.

He never wrote a book, and yet all the libraries of the country could not hold the books that have been written about Him. He never wrote a song, and yet He has furnished the theme for more songs than all the songwriters combined.

He never founded a college, but all the schools put together cannot boast of having as many students.

He never marshalled an army, nor drafted a soldier, nor fired a gun; and yet no leader ever had more volunteers who have, under His orders, made more rebels stack arms and surrender without a shot fired.

He never practiced psychiatry, and yet He has healed more broken hearts than all the doctors far and near.

Once each week the wheels of commerce cease their turning and multitudes wind their way to worshiping assemblies to pay homage and respect to Him.

The names of the past proud statesmen of Greece and Rome have come and gone. The names of the past scientists, philosophers, and theologians have come and gone; but the name of this Man abounds more and more.[5]

In sharing this tribute with a friend recently, he responded, "What you are saying is Jesus is irresistible!"

Just Between Kings

"I know men, and I tell you that Jesus Christ is no mere man," declared Napoleon Bonaparte (1769–1821). He expressed this conviction toward the end of his life with an officer, who joined him in exile. Napoleon, the one-time military genius and self-crowned emperor, went on to compare his legacy to that of Jesus:

Everything in Christ astonishes me. His spirit overawes me, and His will confounds me . . . He is truly a being by Himself. His ideas and sentiments, the truth which He announces, His manner of convincing, are not explained either by human organization or by the nature of things. Alexander, Caesar, Charlemagne, and I have founded empires. But on what did we rest the creations of our genius? Upon force. Jesus Christ alone founded His empire upon love; and at this hour millions of men would die for Him.[6]

When you read a confession like this, it gives new meaning to the title of Jesus "King of kings."

Now He Belongs to the World

It's been said that Jesus is far too important a figure in history just to be left to the consideration of theologians. In a real sense, He belongs to people everywhere, no matter what their race or creed. Theologian Hans Küng shares that Jesus:

is obviously still for innumerable people the most moving figure in the long history of mankind: unusual and incomprehensible in many respects. He is the hope of revolutionaries and evolutionaries, he fascinates intellectuals and anti-intellectuals . . . He constantly stimulates theologians and even atheists to think again.[7]

Jesus Was My Brother

This century has witnessed a flood of books by Jewish authors which accept the cultural Jesus but stop short of acknowledging the religious Jesus. Sholem Asch (1880–1957) was one such author, with books in both Yiddish and English. In his opinion:

Jesus Christ is the outstanding personality of all time . . . No other teacher—Jewish, Christian, Buddhist, Mohammedan—is still a teacher whose teaching is such a guidepost for the world we live in. Other teachers may have something basic for an Oriental, an Arab, or an Occidental; but every act and word of Jesus has value for all of us.[8]

When criticized over his sympathetic view of Jesus, Asch responded, "He became the Light of the World. Why shouldn't I, a Jew, be proud of that?" It is quite likely that more Jews in the future will struggle to acknowledge Jesus as a great Jew, even as a great prophet of Israel.

Jesus Meets Ghandi

Although a devout Hindu, Mahatma Ghandi expressed the deepest admiration for Jesus' teachings and showed how they could be applied to the most far-reaching human problems. "To me he was one of the greatest teachers humanity has ever had," confessed Ghandi.

Ghandi even urged his fellow Hindus to study the teachings of Jesus and was prepared to recognize Jesus as a "son of God" in a different light.

To his believers he was God's only begotten son. Could the fact that I do or do not accept this belief have any more or less influence in my life? Is all the grandeur of his teaching and his doctrine to be forbidden to me? I cannot believe so . . . My interpretation . . . is that Jesus' own life is the key to his nearness to God; that he expressed, as no other could, the spirit and will of God. It is in this sense that I see and recognize him as the son of God.[9]

The Mystery of the Ages

"Though we once regarded Christ from a human viewpoint, we do so no longer," wrote the apostle Paul (2 Corinthians 5:16). Before his conversion, the former persecutor saw Jesus only from a human viewpoint. After his encounter with the risen One, this apostle of faith saw Jesus as much more, as Lord and Christ.

After God made Jesus Lord and Messiah through the resurrection, it was impossible for Paul to consider Him just a man, limited to time and space.

He now saw Christ as putting the world back together into one sacred building. His mission, in turn, was preaching these "unsearchable riches" of Christ to the Gentile nations.

As the early Church received the apostles' teaching they found this treasure of Christ to be inexhaustible. In the letter of the Hebrews, Jesus was already the heavenly high priest. Under the guidance of the Holy Spirit, Christ grew to the length, breadth and depth of the Roman empire.

Still, as Vincent Donovan writes, "Christ is essentially a mystery and can never be fully understood, and certainly never completely defined by a word or concept in any culture. Every age has the right to further exploration and discovery of the meaning of that mystery."[10]

For much of the church, however, this quest to mine the "unsearchable riches" of Christ has ceased. Therefore, the mystery of Christ still remains a mystery for much of the world. As we look again toward Jesus in light of the year 2000, it's time to unwrap history's greatest treasure and invite every people, creed and culture to share in this bimillennial tribute to Christ.

Worship His Majesty

Our attraction is not to the *times* of 2000 but to its *treasure*. The year 2000 is just another year, but there will never be another Jesus. Our desire is for the person of Christ, who has been exalted to the highest place and given the name that is above every name (Philippians 2:9). If this man has indeed been exalted and honored by God, then He deserves every ounce of tribute ever given to Him. There is no way we could ever over praise Him during the bimillennial.

Nothing is so right than giving honor to one to whom honor is due. Rightfully so the world will honor the memory of Jesus in light of the 2,000th anniversary of His birth. As followers of Jesus, however, we have something more to celebrate.

We will honor not only His memory, but worship His majesty. The first relates to the person of Christ, the second to His lordship over this world. Rightfully understood, *Anno Domini* 2000 speaks of the first 2,000 years of the reign of our Lord. As we celebrate the year 2000, we anticipate the greater and fuller reign of Christ's kingdom for ages to come. His is an ever increasing kingdom, a government of which there will be no end! Hallelujah!

It's About Him, Not Us

It's time we ask ourselves the question, "Who is Christ?" Everything else is off the subject. We must measure ourselves against Christ, not measure Him against our churches or our doctrines. Christ, not the institutional church, needs to be the focal point of our journey toward A.D. 2000.

When it comes down to it, the bimillennial of 2000 is about Jesus. It will be a time to develop a new vision of Christ, and ask ourselves how we might measure up to that vision in the new century.

The bimillennial will not be the occasion to point out the achievements, or shortcomings of the Christian era since the birth of Jesus. Fortunately, that time of reckoning comes later in the year 2033, when we celebrate the 2,000th birthday of the church.

Jaroslav Pelikan reminds us that while the prestige of institutional Christianity gradually declined in this second millennium, paradoxically, "the stature of Jesus as an individual increased and his reputation spread."

Jesus once said, "If I be lifted up from the earth, I will draw all men to myself" (John 12:32).

I believe we are about to witness a God-given awakening of interest in the person of Jesus as we move toward the year 2000.

You don't have to be rich to be generous . . .
a pauper can give like a prince.
—Corinne Wells

3

Something Beautiful for God

Mary kept her plan secret, all to herself. It almost spilled out as she helped Martha prepare for the special evening in honor of Jesus. "Martha probably wouldn't approve anyway," Mary thought. She began to reminisce how she received the dowry from her late father. It was worth a huge sum of money, about $20,000 in today's currency. But Mary's heart told her what she should do.

As usual, Martha took charge of the preparations. Six days before the Passover, Jesus arrived in Bethany. The evening finally came. All gathered at Simon's house for a feast.

Just days before, God had indeed worked mightily through Jesus to raise Lazarus from the dead. When the people from Bethany heard Jesus was back in town, they flocked around Simon's house, eager to get a glimpse of Jesus, and Lazarus, who had come back from the grave.

Extravagant Devotion

During an interlude in the meal, Mary unveiled her plan. Out of extravagant devotion to Jesus, she took her alabaster jar of very expensive perfume and poured it on the head of Jesus, and wiped His feet with her hair. The house quickly filled with the fragrance of this imported perfume.

This lavish display of thanksgiving did not go unnoticed. Some of Jesus' disciples were offended and indignantly said to one another, "Why this waste of perfume? It could have been sold for more than a year's wages and the money given to the poor." They began to rebuke Mary harshly.

But Jesus, being deeply moved by Mary's unparalleled devotion, came to her defense. "Leave her alone," said Jesus. "Why are you bothering her? She has a done beautiful thing to me" (Mark 14:6).

When we think about the great saints of the early church we normally lift up great leaders like the apostle Peter or Paul. But on this night, a plain woman touched the heart of Christ. It wasn't the disciples who ministered to Jesus' needs, but Mary, who anointed His body for burial. This simple woman, who probably never preached a sermon or opened the eyes of the blind, made history for all eternity.

Give Him Your All

Mary's tribute was extravagant. But notice how Jesus received it. He said, "Wherever the gospel is preached throughout the world, what she has done will also be told, in memory of her" (Mark 14:9).

I believe it's time again to do something beautiful for God. In the spirit of Mary of Bethany, it's time to arise and pour our gifts on Jesus. Let's fill the earth with the fragrance of our devotion. Don't let your desire be quenched by those who say it's a waste of time and money to honor Jesus so excessively. His bimillennial hour will not always be with us.

How can we walk in the anointing of Mary of Bethany? Here are three starting points.

First, we need to spend time at the feet of Jesus. We seem to always find Mary there in the Gospels, looking at the face of Jesus and listening to His word. I love the prayer of king David, "One thing I ask of the Lord, this is what I seek; that I may dwell in the house of the Lord all the days of my life, to gaze upon the beauty of the Lord and to seek him in his temple" (Psalm 27:4). As we look to the bimillennial, we need to choose the better way of Mary, over the activism of Martha. If we are to give Him our greatest gift, our hearts must be enlarged.

Second, we need to see the material things of life the way God sees them. Mary could have seen the costly spikenard perfume as her possession. It was her rightful inheritance. What woman wouldn't want to save that kind of family heirloom, that kind of perfume, for her wedding? Instead Mary saw her treasure as a gift for God. What have you put away for a rainy day in your "alabaster box" that can be given to God?

Third, like Mary, we need to be in synch with the special seasons in Jesus' life. The dinner at Bethany was held the night before Jesus' passion week began. Somehow, Mary was so intimate with her Lord she knew when Jesus needed encouragement. Sure enough, that night, Jesus was renewed to finish the course laid before Him, which meant embracing the cross.

As we enter the bimillennial era of Jesus, our prayer needs to be: "Lord, help me set my heart to bring you a worthy gift, in honor of your 2,000th anniversary."

A Great Year Coming

This awareness that the year 2000 would be a special season for Christ has been growing for almost twenty years. During this time many groups have been quietly planning to present a gift to God by the year 2000.

This desire first emerged among the "born-again" evangelical movement in the United States. In *Christianity Today's* 1975 opening issue, the editorial team decided to float a trial balloon on the year 2000. Playing off the interest in the upcoming American bicentennial, they ran a cover story entitled, "The Bimillennial: A Great Year Coming."

Managing editor David Kucharsky wrote: "Regardless of whether one embraces the theological Jesus, it is hard to dispute the fact that Jesus was the most important and influential person who has ever lived. On that basis alone the world should find him worthy of a momentous anniversary tribute." At the heart of the bimillennial celebrations surrounding 2000, Kucharsky felt there should be a magnificent Christian observance.

"There's really not a lot of time. We're now at the fourth quarter of this century," Kucharsky noted. "We should not allow the bimillennial to go the way of our Christmas celebration, with its materialistic and pagan accretions."

Kucharsky then proposed that the church should "seize and retain the cultural initiative" and thereby "find many natural 'openings' through which to present the gospel understandably and meaningfully." Back then, *Christianity Today's* trial balloon received less response than anticipated, Kucharsky now admits. Yet beneath the surface, the awareness of Christ's bimillennial was working its way through the entire Christian world.

The First Convert
In 1976, the bimillennial found its first major convert among the Southern Baptists. In keeping with their evangelical zeal, they launched a plan "to reach every living person in the world with the gospel by the year 2000." Dubbed "Bold Mission Thrust" this daring and detailed strategy called for a tenfold increase of churches worldwide by the year 2000.

Historically, the Southern Baptists have always put a priority on foreign missions. So setting a 25-year goal to tackle the world is second nature.

By the mid-'80s, most of the indicators in the Baptists' plan for the year 2000 were ahead of schedule, but the world looked a whole lot larger than it did in 1976!

It was then that Dr. Keith Parks, who at the time was president of their mission board, decided it was time to stop going it alone. In a dramatic series of events from 1985 to 1989, the Southern Baptists opened their doors to new partnerships with other Christian groups, and with governments overseas that traditionally had been hostile to western development workers. Instead of trying to achieve their own agenda, Parks began asking the question, "How can we help you? We want to do anything we can to encourage what God is doing among all of us."

When the first "convert" to the year 2000 among major religious groups starts thinking about how they can be a gift to others, you know a new chapter in history is being written!

A New Advent

But for the untimely death of a newly elected pope in 1978, the Roman Catholic Church may have never joined the movement toward the year 2000. On October 16th, a replacement, Cardinal Karol Wojtyla of Poland, was elected as the first non-Italian pope since 1522.

As he opened his inaugural address the following day, Pope John Paul II acknowledged his sovereign placement in the chair of St. Peter in Rome and declared that the year 2000 "will be the year of a great Jubilee."

He spoke of how the year 2000, in itself, would surely reawaken in people their special awareness of how God dwelt among humanity through Jesus Christ. And he called for the remaining years of the second millennium to be a new advent season for the church and the world at large.

As the 1980s began, the world watched with amazement as this new pope, with his magnetic personality, lifted the hopes and dreams of millions through his world travels. Yet few observers took this year 2000 call seriously. They reasoned, "Hadn't every pope within memory since the year 1300 proclaimed a century's end as some kind of Holy Year?"

But quietly some within the church began to pray that God would bring forth life from the seed that had been sown.

By 1987, this tiny bimillennial seed had become a healthy plant and broke through the crust of the Roman Catholic bureaucracy. Private groups within the church announced a multi-million dollar project called Evangelization 2000 in response to Pope John Paul II's call for a "New Evangelization in anticipation of the year 2000."

Conceived in 1984 by Father Tom Forrest, a leader among charismatic Catholics, Evangelization 2000 set out to instill a new zeal among Catholics to share their faith with others. By the time the Catholic Church launched its "Worldwide Decade of Evangelization" on Christmas Day in 1990, Tom Forrest's evangelizers had:

◆ Rallied more than 4,000 religious orders in an around-the-clock worldwide prayer campaign,

◆ Conducted two worldwide retreats for priests in Rome, drawing 10,000 leaders,

◆ Published 13 issues of *New Evangelization 2000*, a news magazine translated in more than five languages to a readership of 100,000 and

◆ Forged a worldwide network of television producers.

"The year 2000 will be the most extraordinary commemorative event in Christian history. It offers a challenge that calls for a historic Catholic and Christian response," says Forrest. "Our object is to give Jesus Christ a 2,000th birthday gift of a world more Christian than not!"

We are living in incredible times! If this is a sign of things to come, who can tell what will happen in and through the Roman Catholic Church as we approach the bimillennial year of Jesus—A.D. 2000.

The Lord's Pentagon Takes Aim

As Roman Catholics geared up to "evangelize the baptized" in the late '70s, another kind of wheel started to turn among conservative evangelicals in regards to the year 2000. This time, the call to action came from a bald, mild-mannered professor and former missionary named Ralph D. Winter.

In 1976, Dr. Winter began to purchase a college campus in Pasadena, Calif., which he christened the U.S. Center for World Mission—a mission "pentagon" where the Lord's forces could develop and execute joint projects. Winter's burden was to reach the "hidden people"—those pockets of people without an internal Christian witness.

Like a cruise missile locked onto its target, Winter felt Christian agencies should set their sights on reaching specific unreached groups by 2000, rather than aim their resources indiscriminately among people that have already heard the Good Word.

Things seemed to crystalize in 1979 when Winter and his associates came up with a watchword, "A Church for Every People by the Year 2000." To Winter, a Caltech graduate and engineer, this slogan was God-given—it was biblical, strategic, and measurable. Winter was giving a standard "work smarter, not harder" pitch.

"I believe it would be a tragedy if the year 2000 were to become identified merely with small goals," Winter would later state. "Small goals may be good. Denominational goals are good . . . But, in fact, God has given us much larger goals by which all smaller goals are to be judged."[1]

Within 18 months, Winter and his associates used their new year 2000 watchword as a trumpet to gather a world consultation of missionary leaders.

They met in Edinburgh, Scotland, in November 1980, to consider how to direct gospel resources from overevangelized countries, and channel them to those people beyond the range of present outreach.

Let Them See Jesus
By the late '70s, Dr. Bill Bright, the founder of Campus Crusade for Christ, had worked for "the fulfillment of the great

commission" for almost 30 years. On behalf of the church worldwide, Campus Crusade had launched a series of monumental evangelistic projects such as Explo '72 in Dallas, Explo '74 in Seoul, Korea and Here's Life World. In 1979, they took another giant step to help reach the world for Christ.

In November of that year, Campus Crusade released the *JESUS* film, directed by John Hayman, a two-hour motion picture based on the life of Christ from the Gospel of Luke.

The movie premiered in 250 cities across the United States. Within five days Warner Brothers knew it would be a success. Crowds had to be turned away in twenty cities. The classic Cinema in Westcliff, England reported 10,000 attendance in four weeks time. "*JESUS* outdraws E.T," the local papers proclaimed. By the end of its commercial run in theatres, over four million people had witnessed the life of Jesus.

After seeing *JESUS*, a 16-year old in former communist Albania wrote: "Though I am a Muslim girl, I can say that this film was wonderful. I am so excited that I can't put into words what I feel. Jesus gives hope to my hopeless people."

Convinced that Jesus is welcomed where religion is not, Campus Crusade began to grapple with the logistics to insure that every person worldwide could hear the story of Christ in their mother tongue by the year 2000. In the spring of 1980, the *JESUS* film began to be translated into the 390 languages, and 1,000 dialects needed to reach 98% of the world's population, through movie theaters, on television, on video, or 16mm film screenings in rural settings.

After a global satellite conference, called Explo '85, Campus Crusade combined the *JESUS* film with their proven training in evangelism and discipleship into a plan called "New Life 2000." Dr. Billy Graham volunteered to serve as the honorary chairman for what he called, "one of the greatest evangelistic efforts in the history of modern times."

Working in cooperation with national leaders and churches of practically every denomination, New Life 2000 set goals to:

- Help present the gospel to more than 6 billion people by the year 2000.
- Help introduce 1 billion people to Jesus Christ as Lord and Savior.
- Establish 5 million New Life Groups to disciple 200 million new believers.
- Assist denominations to begin 1 million new churches.

Just as Christ miraculously fed the five thousand, only after having His disciples seat the crowd in plots of 50, so New Life 2000 sectioned the world into "million person target areas."

Within these 5,000 target areas, Training Centers began to operate, and *JESUS* film teams were formed. By the end of 1993, some aspect of the New Life 2000 strategy was present in 161 countries, directed by the Campus Crusade team of more than 100,000 staff and trained volunteers. A worldwide electronic tracking system was even in place to monitor progress at 30-day intervals!

In speaking for New Life 2000, Bright said, "By faith, we intend to celebrate not only the birth of Jesus in the year 2000, but the fulfillment of His great commission."

Is God Trying to Tell Us Something?

As different groups sought to do something beautiful for God by the year 2000, a Chinese evangelist by the name of Thomas Wang stepped on the scene.

As the newly appointed International Director of the Lausanne movement, Wang noticed that major denominations and ministries worldwide were beginning to launch A.D. 2000 outreach programs.[2]

On the evening of February 26, 1987, Wang worked late into the evening on an article for the June issue of Lausanne's bi-monthly magazine. At three o'clock in the morning, he paused and said to himself, "My, what is the Lord doing? So many groups are simultaneously beginning to talk about the year 2000. What is happening? What is God trying to say?"

Wang selected eight of the most prominent denominations and mission agencies who where creating gigantic evangelism plans on a global scale. In his article, "By the Year 2000: Is God Trying to Tell Us Something?" he wrote: "I think if only one or two of them succeed in all their objectives, they would truly turn the world upside-down."

Throughout the summer and fall of 1987, thousands of evangelicals around the world read Wang's article with great interest. By year's end, leaders from more than 40 nationalities had written back to confirm his convictions. As Wang would later say, "I hear a bell ringing in heaven, telling us, 'Gentlemen, it's time to get serious. It's time to get together.'"

By mid-1989, Wang formed the AD 2000 Movement, a global coalition of evangelicals to offer the gift of Christ to every person by the year 2000. As of 1991, they had sponsored inter-denominational consultations in 50 countries.

A Holy Council for a Holy Year

The bimillennial has also been an inspiration among ecumenically-minded Christians, who saw their movement make incredible strides toward unity in modern times through the World Council of Churches.

Intending to build on these accomplishments, in 1979, Reformed professor Lew Mudge of San Francisco proposed that the churches which are still divided should settle their remaining differences as we approach the year 2000 and convene a holy council in that year—the first universal church council since A.D. 787. What a gift to God that would be!

Representatives of churches would come from every corner of the earth and all of Christianity's 160 major traditions. It would be the greatest Christian congress in 2,000 years!

Dr. Lukas Vischer, ecumenical officer of the Swiss Reformed Church, describes the council in this way:

> On the opening day of the assembly they would all unite in confession of one and the same apostolic faith

on the basis of years of thorough preparation. They would declare the divisions between them to be a thing of the past and then join together in celebration of the Eucharist. The way would then be open to turn their attention to the great problems requiring solution and to confront the forces threatening humanity and the world with destruction.[3]

Since 1980, many others have issued separate but similar calls for a universal holy council in the year of 2000, but the proposals have yet to turn into public plans.

Carry the Light

While the flame may yet burn brighter in the quest for church unity by the year 2000, the flame is already blazing across the world among a new generation of youth, especially among charismatic Christians.

In 1988, on Easter Sunday in Jerusalem, an Olympic-style torch was lit and carried by 20 young runners to Tel Aviv. The next day, it was flown by plane on a special charter to Finland and from there lit torches that fanned out to every region of the world. Since that time, more than 500,000 youth worldwide have participated in the "Target 2000 Torch Run."

Organized in relay teams, they have run the length and breadth of their country, or across their city. Youth With a Mission organizers claim it is their way to fire the imagination and dreams of tomorrow's leaders to "carry the light" of Jesus so it might shine in every heart by the year 2000.

"The 25-year-old missionary of the year 2000 is already 19 years old today," claimed Floyd McClung, one of the international Torch Run organizers. "I see this Torch Run like the passing of a baton. Before you get to the person you are to hand the baton to you say, 'Go.' We need to begin saying 'go' to thousands of youth worldwide now." The Torch Run has particularly been used to inspire faith at massive rallies, outreaches, and congresses.

The Decade of Power Evangelism

In August of 1990, former Olympic track star Jim Ryun carried the torch the last leg of a 6,500-mile run into the Hoosier Dome in Indianapolis where 23,000 people gathered for the "North American Congress on the Holy Spirit and World Evangelization." This five-day festival marked the second time since 1986 that charismatic Christians, who stress the power and presence of the Holy Spirit, gathered to specifically launch the "Decade of Evangelization, 1991–2000."

Dr. Vinson Synan, organizer of the North American Congress points out that the Pentecostal movement among Christians "actually began on the very first day of this century, January 1, 1900, in Topeka, Kansas."

As Synan looks to the year 2000, he sees the charismatic movement ready to close this century with the greatest decade in Christian history, filled with signs and wonders, miracles, healings and power evangelism.

Synan is not just exaggerating. The worldwide charismatic and Pentecostal movement has more than tripled in the last decade to 372 million, making it the second largest family of Christians worldwide.

A New Wind Is Blowing

What is the significance of so many groups preparing something beautiful for God by the year 2000?

The Holy Spirit is awakening within hearts everywhere a desire to honor Jesus with an extraordinary gift during His bimillennial era. These dramatic developments lead me to believe that this invitation to Christ's celebration 2000 originated in heaven itself!

The Spirit of God is indeed blowing across our world as we move toward the year 2000. You can sit back and say, "So what?" Or you can pull in your oars, hoist up your sail and capture the divine breeze pointed toward Christ's special season of 2000.

Let's go to Bethlehem and see
this thing that has happened.
—Luke 2:15

4

The Reason
for the Season

"Bah! Humbug!" old Scrooge said to his nephew. "What's so merry about Christmas?" Charles Dickens created some of the most famous characters in English literature, but none more memorable than Ebenezer Scrooge. On Christmas Eve, this unpleasant old miser scorns the Christmas spirit. But after visits from the ghosts of Christmas past, present and future, his life is forever changed. After this, he lived the Christmas spirit not only at Christmas time but all year long. Since 1843, Dicken's immortal tale, *A Christmas Carol*, has become one the most famous stories ever written.

The Spirit of Christmas
Jesus' bimillennial in 2000 will touch anyone who still believes in the power of the first Christmas story. For it is this original Christmas event, the birth of the Christ Child, that lies at the heart of the bimillennial commemorations.

December 25, 2000, will no doubt be celebrated as the most memorable Christmas ever. As early as 1987, the Roman Catholic Church talked about ten-year preparations needed for a worldwide satellite telecast on Christmas Day in the year 2000. Pope John Paul II or his successor is scheduled to speak to a potential audience of 5 billion people.

In addition to the Vatican, other global commemorations of Christ will likely be organized in historic places such as Bethlehem, Nazareth and Jerusalem.

Instead of the Christmas season in 1999 lasting from Thanksgiving to Christmas Day, the world will likely celebrate an entire Christmas year leading up to December 25, 2000. Think of it as an official year-long celebration of Christmas, from December 25, 1999 to Christmas Day 2000.

An Entire Year of Christmas

Celebrations of Jesus' bimillennial will last far more than the 12 days of Christmas, but continue for 12 months of Christmas, becoming a historic "World Christmas Year."

Early signs of this world Christmas year could appear well before 2000, including possibilities I've dreamed up like:

> *TV Guide, 1996*: Tonight the Turner Entertainment Network will premier the first of a ten-part series on Jesus of Nazareth, designed as a 2,000th anniversary tribute to the impact of his life, ethics, and legacy on world civilization.

> *The ITAR Tass News Agency, 1997*: Not since the 1957 launch of Sputnik has Russia caught the attention of the world by the launch of a satellite. Today the space agency will launch a "Star of Hope" satellite as a global symbol of good will and understanding. The 500-pound package will be a solar-powered signal light, visible to the naked eye as it circles the globe. President Gaidar said, "In commemoration of the star of Bethlehem, this is a beacon of hope, a call to all people to follow the path of peace."

The Washington Post, 1998: In anticipation of the biggest Christmas in 2,000 years, the Christian Broadcasting Network announced plans today to cover live, via simulcast, the global Christmas Eve celebrations being planned in 24 time zones for December 24, 2000.

Time magazine, 1999: Rather than name a person of the year, we have decided to name the Man of the Millennium: Jesus Christ. Regardless of whether one embraces the theological Jesus, it is hard to dispute the fact that Jesus has been the most important, the most influential, and certainly the most intriguing, person of the last two-thousand years.

With these developments, or ones similar, the world Christmas year of 2000 will likely commemorate both the original Christmas story and our shared Christmas culture.

In the year 2000, concert halls in cities worldwide will likely feature performances of Handel's *Messiah* or Bach's *Christmas Oratorio*. Special exhibits in art museums will celebrate the paintings of Christ, such as Raphael's "The Sistine Madonna." Theatres will be filled with productions such as "The Promise" or "Jesus Was His Name."

Libraries will celebrate the literature of the Christmas season, such as Dickens' five Christmas books, or the 1882 classic poem "The Night Before Christmas." Publishers will release coffee table books on the life of Jesus. And television producers will rerun "The Miracle on 34th Street" to celebrate the bimillennial spirit.

In addition, bimillennial commissions will likely sponsor writing contests and issue magazines, commemorative coins, memorabilia or stamps.

Nativity plays and Christmas choir concerts will likely appear year-round in churches.

Religious pilgrims by the millions will stream to historic places associated with Jesus' life in the Holy Land. The travel

industry will offer vacations during the world Christmas year
to historic Christian centers such as Rome, Istanbul, Moscow
or London. The 2,000th anniversary of the birth of Christ will
be the greatest Christmas ever!

The Great Omission

Recently I ran across what I consider to be the first scholarly
book on the bimillennial. With delight I spent an evening
poring through the pages of *Celebrations* by William Johnston.[1]
It was thorough. I kept reading . . . it was a virtual gold mine
on the modern age of anniversaries. Surely I would find mention of Jesus' bimillennial.

I kept reading. Rather than just one paragraph on the
bimillennial, it had three chapters. One was even titled,
"Christian Anniversaries in a Secular Age." I read on. The book
closed with a rundown on the major anniversaries of late 1990s.
But it completely overlooked Jesus' 2,000th birthday!

The next morning I dashed off a letter to the author and
asked: "Was it an oversight, or just an omission of the obvious,
that caused you not to mention in your book the upcoming
2,000th anniversary of the birth of Jesus?"

Two weeks later I got his response: "Here I fear I will dis-
appoint you." The author explained that A.D. 2000 would not
be the bimillennial of Jesus since he assumed, as most historians do, that Jesus was born at the latest by 4 B.C., which
would put his bimillennial in 1997.

Johnston is correct, technically that is. But let's go a step
further. It is not uncommon for major anniversaries to be celebrated on days other than their actual dates. We don't even
celebrate George Washington's birthday on the actual anniversary, but rather on the established anniversary date. So it
will be with Jesus' anniversary.

Accurate or not, Jesus' bimillennial almost certainly will
be celebrated the world over in 2000, no matter if modern day
scholars recognize the Christmas season or not.

No Person Can Monopolize?

For many people around the world, Christmas is their most beloved holiday. Several years ago I spent the Christmas holidays in Singapore. I was surprised to see Christmas symbols and decorations everywhere, despite the fact that only 14 percent of the population is Christian. Even if Christmas were just a brief season of good will among men, it would be welcome.

Christmas is far more beautiful than that. Man-made festivals fade, but the life God gives in secret, in humility, endures. If God can indeed dwell among men, as the Scriptures affirm, then from that cradle of eternal love there is hope that civilization's highest visions might be fulfilled.

Is it presumptuous to believe that the life once given in Bethlehem square might still serve as a guiding vision over what some call our modern-day "naked public squares"?

Christians cannot presume they will be the only ones celebrating 2000, but all of society should be aware that the roots of 2000 tap deeply into Christ.

Johnston doubts whether any one person or group can unify major mega-anniversaries in our postmodern era. Even though the world lives under the banner of our common civil Great Calendar with its predictable anniversaries, a vacuum of values threatens to subvert any single conviction or predominate mega-image. He writes:

> I predict that efforts . . . to focus the bimillennial will be only partly successful because too many other groups will seize the initiative to impose shape on the amorphousness of this super-anniversary. The appeal of the cult of anniversaries is that each one supplies its own agenda, as we saw with the Columbus year. Even that lost shape as the year proceeded. The shapelessness of the bimillennial will be even more apparent, come the Year 2000 . . . My inference from studying recent commemorations is that no person or group can preempt or monopolize an event like 2000.[2]

This observation is a clear wake-up call, not just to the church, but to anyone who believes that society ought to have a common vision of the common good. The reality Johnston describes is "countercommemorations." Not only do today's cultural managers use major anniversaries to celebrate every nuance of opinion, but cultural critics particularly "aim to reshape offerings of the Great Calendar into counter images of official agendas."

This struggle to bring meaning to the cultural symbols of society was all too apparent during the quincentennial.

Do We Protest or Parade?

Recently I saw a bumper sticker which summarized the fault lines that surfaced in the quincentennial. It read, "Discover Columbus' Legacy: 500 years of racism, oppression, & stolen land." Unfortunately in 1992, most Americans or Europeans didn't know whether to protest or parade.

Sadly, even the churches were divided as they entered the quincentennial. Two years before the 500th anniversary of Christopher Columbus in the Americas, mainline Protestant leaders talked about "invasion," "oppression" and "genocide." They called for repentance and reconciliation.

On the other hand, Roman Catholic groups forged ahead with plans for "commemoration" and talk of "evangelization." The rest of us were left in the middle to ask what the quincentennial was really all about. Were we celebrating a continent that was found or mourning an indigenous American civilization that was lost?

In October, 1991, *Time* magazine asked, "Will the hero of 1492 be the villain of 1992?" Even at that early point, the fuss over Columbus threatened to rain on the Rose Parade. Originally, the Pasadena Tournament of Roses Association had chosen Cristóbal Colón, a 20th-generation descendant of Columbus, as the 1992 parade grand marshal.

After an onslaught of Columbus-bashing, the Rose Parade

had second thoughts. They struck a deal. Colón would only be a co-grand marshall. He would be joined by Ben Nighthorse Campbell, an American Indian descendant. So on January 1, 1992, Colón in a carriage, and Campbell on his horse, alternated in the lead of the Rose Parade, each man free to receive applause or boos.

Whatever our perspective on 1492, mega-anniversaries should not be designated as a battleground for cultural war. We must do better for the bimillennial. A way must be found for the whole world to appreciate "the reason for the season."

The Man Nobody Knows

Much of the quest to define the bimillennial will pivot on how people, Christian or otherwise, relate to Jesus as a cultural symbol. It is obvious that Jesus stands in relationship to the bimillennial in the same way that Columbus did to the quincentennial.

In contrast to the character discussions about whether Columbus was obsessed by gold or God, whether he was a saint or a womanizer, explorer or exploiter—no serious person would dare question the character of Christ.

There will always be the sensational author or movie claiming that Jesus didn't die on the cross or was secretly married to Mary Magdalene. This kind of "creativity" with the Gospel narratives has never stuck to Christ.

Despite the fact there is more historical evidence of Jesus' existence than any other person of antiquity, others might go so far to assert that Jesus never lived. In 1970, John Allegro, a British specialist of Oriental studies, argued this case in all seriousness in *The Sacred Mushroom and the Cross*. In his opinion, Christianity began as a secret cult of the sacred mushroom and "Jesus" was a code word for hallucinators.

Because the historical testimony is so strong against them, allegations like these are best ignored, lest by our opposition they draw strength from the publicity. Counter-images like these are merely proof of the continuing fascination Jesus exercises on people's minds.

As we approach the bimillennial, there should be no need for anyone to defend Jesus' character. He has endured the test of time and He will continue to do so.

Even outside the church, there is an enormous respect and reverence toward Jesus. The vast majority of modern literary portrayals of Jesus are by no means lacking in aesthetic quality or theological depth.

The bimillennial will be a first-class opportunity for society to take another look at Jesus. This must become an occasion where the church extends an open hand, not a closed fist, to those who see in Jesus the highest and best ideals.

Even though we believe Jesus is the Son of God, we must confess that we have not yet fully mined the treasures that His life presents. At times, the world can reveal a broader implication of the gospel of Jesus Christ which the church has forgotten or never discovered.

The Incredible Shrinking Jesus

Others may register no complaints about the celebrations of Jesus' bimillennial. They will merely point out that the commemorations have more to do with the Christ of faith than the Jesus of history.

For two hundred years, many New Testament scholars were occupied with the "Quest for the Historical Jesus." They approached the Gospels with a critical eye to peel away the supposed miracle myths that the church created around Jesus—the "peasant revolutionary."

The quest to weigh every saying of Jesus to determine its historical validity began to collapse when scholars pointed out that very often a person's predisposition against the supernatural can shape their findings as much as the tools of literary analysis.

By the time the "death of God" debate dead-ended in the

'60s it became clear the "minimized" Jesus also wasn't worth keeping.

In volume three of *The Story of Civilization*, historian Will Durant summarized his conclusions about Jesus and history:

> That a few simple men should in one generation have invented so powerful and appealing a personality, so lofty an ethic and so inspiring a vision of human brotherhood, would be a miracle far more incredible than any recorded in the Gospels. After two centuries of higher criticism the outlines of the life, character, and teaching of Christ remain reasonably clear, and constitute the most fascinating feature in the history of Western man.[3]

Today, many scholars feel the Jesus of history and the Christ of faith overlap considerably.

Old arguments, even though largely resolved, have a strange resilient currency. The "historical Jesus" may resurface again as we approach the bimillennial, but it should not define our ground rules to assess His life and legacy.

Education Precedes Celebration

A recurring criticism of the United States bicentennial in 1976 was that it promoted celebration without education. The result, one observer wrote with sorrow, was that Americans were left with little more than "tons of red-white-and-blue junk, that made advertisers and commercial hucksters rich, but neither enriched the spirit nor nourished the understanding of the American people."[4]

We should determine from the start that this will not be the case with the bimillennial of Jesus' birth. Education needs to precede celebration which, in turn, should lead to rededication.

Well before the global year of Christmas in 2000, education should emphasize the relevance of Christ's whole life and the enduring power of His legacy in civilization.

The Enduring Legacy of Jesus

As people prepared a hundred years ago to celebrate the turn of the century, the most popular book of the day was about life in the year 2000. It's true. Edward Bellamy's *Looking Backwards, 2000–1887* sold more than ten million copies. This utopian novel told the story of Julian West, who fell asleep in Boston, only to wake up in 2000 to discover a near perfect world.

Later, Bellamy continued the story of Julian West for the *Ladies Home Journal*. In this short piece of fiction entitled "Christmas in the year 2000," West describes how Christmas is now celebrated as "the world's great emancipation day and feast of all liberties." West then contrasted this with the pathetic personal celebrations of Christmas in the 19th century, which observed Jesus' birth through mere family reunions.

We must not lose sight of the fact that Jesus brought about the greatest social revolution the world has ever seen and His work continues.

Poet Howard Thurman underscores this in his poem, "The Work of Christmas."

> When the song of the angels is stilled,
> When the star in the sky is gone,
> When the kings and princes are home,
> When the shepherds are back with their flock,
> The work of Christmas begins:
> To find the lost,
> To heal the broken,
> To feed the hungry,
> To release the prisoner,
> To rebuild the nations,
> To bring peace among others,
> To make music in the heart.[5]

© 1973 Howard Thurman. Used by permission.

We must ask ourselves, "How can the 2,000th anniversary of the birth of Jesus go beyond reinforcing group identity among His followers, to truly call forth renewal within society?"

No person in the history of the world has called forth more study and reassessment than Jesus. After twenty centuries, we are at a unique position to weigh the Nazarene's life, to look with new eyes at the processes He unfolded, to reassess the values and attitudes He fostered in the cultures that followed Him, found both in the West and the East.

We should not lose this opportunity to establish Jesus' place in history and culture.

Come to the Mountaintop

Mountain climbers have learned the wisdom of scaling high peaks in stages. First they establish base camp. Then they successively reach higher levels. Finally they make the climb toward the pinnacle. In a similar way, I sense our climb up Christ's bimillennial mountain will unfold in three phases.

1. Exploration, 1995—1996

Still being uncharted ground for most, these years should call forth much investigation and study of what it would mean for followers of Jesus worldwide to celebrate His 2,000th anniversary.

At base camp, we must ask questions such as, "What does the bimillennial mean?" and "How has society commemorated previous mega-anniversaries?" Let's learn our lesson from the quincentennial. We shouldn't let Jesus' bimillennial lose focus.

Bimillennial consultations should gather theologians, educators, publishers and producers to focus the discussions. Denominations should establish bimillennial commissions among their different departments. Mission groups should consider how their outreach can amplify the commemorative season. Local churches should pray for a clearer vision of Christ and A.D. 2000.

In June 1994, Pope John Paul II convened an extraordinary meeting of the world's Cardinals to ask how the Roman Catholic Church should commemorate the year 2000. This is no doubt the first of many denominational summits from now until 1996 that will turn the eyes of the world toward the mountain peak of Christ and 2000.

2. Preparation, 1997—1998

After mapping the path to the peak of 2000, the church will likely turn her attention to prepare and get outfitted for the journey.

This should become a leading concern among educators worldwide. Look for an unprecedented outpouring of scholarship to be produced on Jesus. In addition, creative short stories, novels, plays, essays, books, symphonies and documentaries will likely be written about Jesus, all reaching its crest by the year 2000 or soon after.

Up until now, most preparations for A.D. 2000 have been primarily cast in terms of a decade of evangelism. Others have turned their countdown to 2000 into annual celebration themes, such as the year of the family, the year of youth, the year of women.

This is all well and good, but we have largely missed the fact that A.D. 2000 points more to Jesus than to the church or its constituencies.[6] Like John the Baptist prepared the way for Jesus, these preliminary strategies will likely give way to preparations for Jesus' celebration.

We need to rediscover Jesus in this decade. It's time for the church to rediscover the reason for the season. By 1997 or 1998, plans for celebration 2000 will likely be unfolding within every major city worldwide.

3. Commemoration, 1999—2001

Before God gave the Ten Commandments, the Scriptures say that Moses and the seventy elders of Israel went up to the mountain "and saw the God of Israel. Under his feet was something like a pavement made of sapphire, clear as the sky itself." Together on the mountain top, "they ate and drank" with God (Exodus 24:9-10). Talk about the ultimate mountain-top experience! Don't stop climbing now, our time is coming!

After the preparation years, the church will climb the pinnacle from 1999-2001. Having arrived at the peak, we will shout to the world, "All things are ready. Come to the mountaintop. The feast is ready to begin!"

The commemorative period of the bimillennial will be full of banquet tables, each with special dishes of food. One dish or event which has already caught the imagination of the media is December 31, 1999. A recent novel, *Millennium's Eve*, describes the drama of a mega-gathering of Christians in Los Angeles. It's an intriguing novel.[7] How often do you get the opportunity to celebrate the biggest New Year's Eve in a thousand years?

The high point of the bimillennial for the church will be Christmas Day 2000, when it commemorates the 2,000th anniversary of the birth of its founder.

But that will not be the end. For on January 1, 2001, we will celebrate the start of the third millennium of the Christian era. Truly kings and prophets longed to see our day!

There is nothing stronger in all the world
than an idea whose time has come.
—Victor Hugo

5

A Powerful Mega-Image

"I see a wrapped gift coming down from heaven!" exclaimed Esther. We were gathered in prayer around our dinner table with some dear Hispanic friends. Apparently, the technicolor scene lasted for just a brief moment. Esther continued, "As this birthday gift was about to touch earth, a multitude of hands reached out to grab it.

"At that moment, the Lord spoke to those with outreached arms and said in Spanish, 'No, este regalo es para mi pueblo,' or 'This gift is for all my people.'" This vision concluded with a scene of vast multitudes walking with raised arms in high praise to God.

Rather than fade with the passing of time, this scene of the heavenly birthday gift has only become more meaningful to me since that evening in March 1989.

To me, the bimillennial means nothing less than a greater presence of the Lord Jesus. This coming gift of Christ is not just for me or my denomination to grab. The gift of Jesus in our times is for the whole church, and ultimately, the whole world.

A Single Great Idea

If the bimillennial season is to be full and powerful, it must be understood through an A.D. 2000 mega-image—a metaphor that springs forth from the person of Christ, and the events surrounding His birth.

It has been said that every movement which has done something great for civilization has had three characteristics. First, it has been bold and has inspired imagination. Second, it built up leadership as it progressed. Third, it has offered a single great idea that was easily grasped and simply shared.

There is no doubt that the year 2000 can stretch the imagination. It has proven that it can attract leadership from all walks of life. What remains to be seen as we move into the bimillennial era is whether the church can offer the world a single great idea, a powerful A.D. 2000 mega-image.

From Megatrends to Mega-Images

In the '80s we got used to thinking about the "megatrends" shaping our lives as we approach the year 2000. Now we must think about what mega-images might best define the drama of this special season.

For the church, the "single great idea" behind the bimillennial is the *single great person* of Jesus. Yet to a large degree, much of the success of the bimillennial era will depend on what images or themes we use to define our journey to Christ.

For an A.D. 2000 mega-image to be useful, it must communicate the bimillennial is:

- for all the people,
- a once-in-a-life time experience and
- a journey toward growth and self-discovery.[1]

In the case of A.D. 2000, many symbols already exist. As leaders who aim to see the bimillennial era point to Christ, we can use these existing mega-images, or develop new ones.

In 1991, my search to find existing A.D. 2000 mega-images took me to the Library of Congress. There I sifted through

hundreds of books with the year 2000 in their title. That was
no small task since more than 2,000 books and 15,000 journal
articles have been published on the year 2000 since 1950. I
carried back home with me a whole suitcase of photocopied
papers. For two years they stayed in one stack.

To make sense of this pile, I finally came up with a fivefold
classification. I call these metaphors the "Five A.D. 2000
Mega-Images." Each one in their own way has shaped how we
have approached the bimillennial over the past 30 years. In a
nutshell they are:

◆   Threshold 2000
◆   Trends 2000
◆   Agenda 2000
◆   Renewal 2000
◆   Jubilee 2000

Our purpose in looking at these images is to weigh each one
and ask, "What does this mega-image offer to the development
of the bimillennial era of Jesus?"

1. Threshold 2000

The first A.D. 2000 mega-image that has been used to shape
the bimillennial is Threshold 2000. This mega-image takes the
year 2000 as the millennium, the 1,000 year rule or reign of
Christ.[2] Whether literally or figuratively, it sees the year 2000
as a cataclysmic shift, a turning point, a tidal wave of global
transformation that will sweep away an old civilization and
usher in a new golden age. The mega-image here is the edge
of a cliff.

This is not a new idea. For more than 500 years, psychics,
seers, pundits and prophets have been transfixed by the year 2000.
Even in modern times, trend watchers, global planners and
futurists have hooked their sights to this guiding star. No other
year in all of human history, before or beyond, has gathered such
incredible prophetic bets as A.D. 2000, given by such luminaries
as Newton to Nostradamus, and Jeane Dixon to Ronald Reagan.

Some swear it will bring doomsday. Others claim it will usher in a utopian age. Either way, those who see 2000 as a threshold date look toward 2000 through millennial lenses.

The year 2000 attracts us for the same reason people have been attracted by millennialism, utopianism or progressivism. We believe that paradise is not behind us, but just ahead, perhaps within our reach, or that of our children. Despite the mess we find ourselves in, we believe in the possibility of global transformation.

But the millennial metaphor is full of tensions. European historian Hillel Schwartz calls it a two-sided coin. Before you get to paradise, you must pass through Armageddon.

The Terminal Generation

The Threshold 2000 mega-image has been particularly attractive to bible teachers. Hal Lindsey's *The Late Great Planet Earth* became the best-selling non-fiction book of the '70s. To date, more than 35 million copies have been sold through more than 113 printings. He convinced millions we were a terminal generation, not due to an environmental apocalypse, but because of a coming nuclear Armageddon.

Lindsey followed this with other prophecy books such as *Countdown to Armageddon*. Lindsey's charts of Christ's second coming have clearly orbited around the nation of Israel and the period from 1988 to the year 2000. While Lindsey never connected all the dots to the year 2000, others have.

About two years ago, I called a businessman I had met to propose we get together for lunch. He was very receptive until I mentioned the year 2000. He immediately clipped back, "We won't be here by 2000. The rapture is coming in '98. I am certain of that. I am publishing a book on the subject."

Later that week, I wrote in my journal: "I would never bet the farm house on the rapture by '98, maybe at most I would bet the barn. On the other hand, betting the farm house on Jesus' celebration 2000 seems much more of a sure thing."

A Dress Rehearsal for the Second Coming?

As a vision of the future, what does the Threshold 2000 mega-image offer the coming bimillennial?

Wrongly applied, a Threshold 2000 mega-image can flat out dismiss the bimillennial, as in my friend's case. At its worst, millennialism can turn into a survival movement, a waiting game, a great escape for the chosen.

At best, a Threshold 2000 mega-image offers us everything! What better culmination to the bimillennial than to have the guest of honor, the Lord Jesus, personally arrive to usher in His kingdom?

It is more likely that the bimillennial will be an approximation of the consummation, rather than the end of the world. Think of it as a dress rehearsal for the second coming. If that's the case, a Threshold 2000 mentality could partially shape the bimillennial in several ways.

+ It can remind us of the destructive forces that were released in the 20th century. Of all centuries, ours has been startled by the possibility of apocalypse. Nations, families and ethnic groups are divided and besieged by chaos and crisis.

+ It can instill in us a hope that out of this decadence, this turbulence, will come rebirth and global renovation under the reign of Christ.

+ It can help us think about history with biblical eyes and language, particularly as humanity ponders the arrival of the third millennium.

2. Trends 2000

The second mega-image used to define the bimillennial era is Trends 2000. Unlike Threshold 2000, a Trends 2000 mega-image highlights continuity, achievement and growth of humankind. If Threshold 2000 peers through millennial lenses, Trends 2000 prefers to view things from mountaintop vistas to put the bimillennial in perspective.

As we near the year 2000, there is an irresistible urge to look backward and then forward, retrospect and prospect. These actions express our human instinct for putting things in order.

Lists will sum up the achievements of the past 2,000 years and chart possibilities for the new epoch. Standing on the summit of 2000, thousands of writers will wet their index fingers, raise them to the sky and see which way the wind is blowing.

In Roman mythology, Janus was the wind god who brought new beginnings. It is no accident that the first month of our year is named January. In most cases, Janus was pictured with two faces, one old which looked to the past with wisdom and one young which looked to the future with idealism. There's no doubt the turn of the millennium will pass in review under both perspectives.

Since we live in an age which has extended both the past and future horizons, the efforts to sum up the past will be monumental, and the attempts to preview the future will be gigantic. In fact, they have already begun.

Mega-Optimist

The best known Trends 2000 book is *Megatrends 2000* by John Naisbitt and Patricia Aburdene. In it they predict ten new directions of the '90s, including the rise of the Pacific Rim, a renaissance of the arts, more women leaders and a religious revival. They include two excellent sections on the year 2000 as the most compelling symbol of our times.[3]

Since its January 1990 release, *Megatrends 2000* has enjoyed phenomenal success, cashing in on the magic of the new millennium. According to Megatrends Limited, this book has been published in 35 countries and enjoyed best-seller status in the United States, Japan, and Germany. It has been released in more than 25 languages including Croatian, Chinese, Korean and Russian.

A Key to Look at History

Not content to just look forward a decade, science fiction writer Isaac Asimov has sought to recap the highlights of human history in the *March of the Millennia*. In his 413th book, and one of his last, he turned his gaze from the stars back to earth to survey the development of civilization, millennium by millennium, beginning in the distant human past of 8000 B.C. and moving forward to the year 2000.

Asimov felt that we "who are the people of the next millennium" ought to think expansively and have "the perspective that humanity, for all the mistakes we have made, has come a long way since the dawn of civilization, and there is a long way yet to go."[4]

The Great Reappraisal Coming

What does a Trends 2000 mega-image offer us as we seek to define the bimillennial era? A Trends 2000 mega-image reminds us that the bimillennial era will be a time for a great reappraisal, in practically every field of learning.

Numerous authors will lean their books up against the year 2000 and claim their expansive works provide the great reappraisal humanity has long awaited. Some of their appraisals may be stretching, or even challenging at points, to traditional theology.

From a holistic perspective, many Trends 2000 mega-images stop short. They cover the ascent of man, but miss the descent of God. The bimillennial must not just celebrate the human story, or the universe story, as important as these may be. It must also celebrate God's story, as made known through Jesus Christ.

The bimillennial will be a natural occasion for the church to rediscover and celebrate Christ as Lord of the whole universe, not just the church. At best, a Trends 2000 approach to the bimillennial era offers a vision of the future, filled with hope rather than fraught with fear.[5]

The Trends 2000 mega-image can likely provide a context to the bimillennial, but probably can not contain the fullness of Christ.

3. Agenda 2000

The third mega-image which has shaped our approach to the bimillennial is Agenda 2000. It sees A.D. 2000 as a milestone date to work toward. It aims to tackle unfinished agendas through setting local, national and global goals. This mega-image is a finish line, calling us to enter the race.

John Naisbitt feels the year 2000 compels us to examine ourselves and resolve our problems so we can meet the new millennium with a clean slate. Those problems we do not willingly confront, it seems, are being thrust upon us.[6]

Agenda 2000 programs usually have one or two horizons. One is an action plan for this decade, the other for a new century. The latter approach asks, "What will be the major, first-intensity issues facing the world as the new century opens?" The former says, "If we are serious about addressing them, how far can we reasonably expect to move along the path toward solutions in the intervening years before 2000?"

By the late '80s, research showed that more than 2,000 groups existed with year 2000 goals. And that number was growing weekly, within government, business, education and religion.

The United Nations alone has many Agenda 2000 programs or agencies working for education 2000, health 2000, transportation 2000, literacy 2000, food 2000, economics 2000, peace 2000, environment 2000, and indigenous peoples 2000. And that is just the short list!

A Strategy to Save Our Planet

Perhaps the most well-known Agenda 2000 program is the Earth Summit Strategy. On June 13th, 1992, nearly 100 world leaders met around a single table in Rio de Janeiro for the largest face-to-face meeting of national leaders in the history of the world.

The main binding agreement, signed by all 172 participating nations, including the United States, was called *Agenda 21*. This was a comprehensive global action plan to confront and overcome the most pressing problems facing our planet.[7]

Virtually every aspect of human civilization was addressed by some portion of this blueprint for action leading up to the next century. *Agenda 21* is organized around seven themes, 40 separate sub-topics of concern are addressed, with 120 separate action plans outlined. The seven central themes are:

◆ The Quality of Life on Earth
◆ Efficient Use of the Earth's Natural Resources
◆ The Protection of our Global Commons
◆ The Management of Human Settlements
◆ Chemicals and the Management of Waste
◆ Sustainable Economic Growth
◆ Implementing *Agenda 21*

The final theme covers the means and methods to implement and monitor the action steps which are relevant to the above six themes.

In the follow-up to *Agenda 21*, a great effort is being undertaken to integrate economic and environment issues to achieve sustainable growth. National governments, United Nation agencies and private organizations are forming concrete action plans to insure that *Agenda 21* is carried out.

The Great Foot Race

Not just world environment, but world evangelism groups have targeted the year 2000. One coalition of evangelicals calls itself the AD 2000 Movement, Inc. Launched in 1989, it took its direction from "the meeting of the century" in Singapore, where 300 Christian leaders gathered to set goals to reach the world for Christ by 2000.

The remarkable thing about the AD 2000 Movement is its predominantly Third World leadership. Its chairman is Chinese, its director is Argentine and its congress director is from India. While being international in leadership, American principles of management guide the AD 2000 Movement's efforts as if it were a Fortune 500 company. The leadership is known for originating terms such as the "10/40 window," and "strategic-level spiritual warfare" to describe their priority targets and methods for evangelism.

Another Agenda 2000 effort is the World Evangelization Database managed by Dr. David Barrett. He and his colleagues publish a regular *AD 2000 Global Monitor* complete with commentary on global mission endeavors and profiles of unevangelized people. Their newsletter's masthead reveals their Agenda 2000 approach: "A monthly trends newsletter measuring progress in world evangelization into the 21st Century."[8]

Barrett has also published the most comprehensive statistics manual for the decade of harvest entitled *Our Globe and How to Reach It*.[9] After reading this book, you get the impression that world evangelization by 2000 could best be compared to a track race. It offers starting-line statistics, finish-line goals for 2000 and a 100-point action plan to improve the stride of global mission groups.

From Need-Driven to Grace-Directed

What do Agenda 2000 programs offer the bimillennial? At best these programs allow us to celebrate the year 2000 in action, not just in thought. They prepare a more just and peaceful world that is worthy of celebration. An evangelized world would be a wonderful gift for the church to present to Christ on the occasion of His 2,000th birthday.

The weakness of some—perhaps many Agenda 2000 programs is the fact they are just that—programs. Most have only shallow or undeveloped images of the future. They may have an image of the present, which is then projected to the year

2000, but few have an image of the future. Mere progress in relation to a list of priorities will not give direction to the bimillennial era on the global level. Targets and goals may move activists, but they alone will not take us beyond ourselves or transform us.

The bimillennial era needs to be grace-directed rather than strategy- or need-driven. What many from a new generation are longing for is a movement of God that takes us all to a place we have never been before.

4. Renewal 2000

Rather than a flat view of A.D. 2000 as a milestone, many have held up the year 2000 as a mirror, in order to see ourselves better. Convinced we have not arrived, Renewal 2000 calls for revival, renovation, restoration and renaissance in light of A.D. 2000. The mega-image here is one of rebirth and experiencing the new millennium through personal and social transformation.

Hosea, the ancient biblical prophet, saw times of refreshment coming to the earth only after God's people repented and came to the point of saying, "Come, let us return to the Lord. He has torn us to pieces but he will heal us . . . After two days he will revive us, on the third day he will restore us that we may live in his presence" (Hosea 6:1-2).

It is as if modern man, on the eve of A.D. 2000, has come to the end of his own resources. Will he, "after two days" cry out for revival? If he does, would not the Lord restore the church on the morning of "the third day," at the dawn of the third millennium?

A Call to Genuine Repentance

One of the most memorable ten days my wife Olgy and I have ever shared was in July 1989, when we joined more than 4,000 Christian leaders from 166 nations in Manila for the "Second International Congress on World Evangelization," sponsored by the Lausanne movement. As this congress was on the eve of the '90s, a great banner was raised to reach the world for Christ by A.D. 2000.

In response to this call to action, Peter Kuzmic, a Croatian theologian, admonished us to pursue Renewal 2000 first, before we launched any Agenda 2000 efforts. "The eloquence of the preacher, the size of the annual budget, the rise of modern technology, the employment of social sciences, effective strategies, top management and impressive missionary agencies and headquarters will not do it," Kuzmic cried out. "It will take genuine repentance, divine cleansing, holy living and a new empowerment by the Holy Spirit if the world is to be evangelized in the last decade of our millennium."[10]

Like seismologists predicting earthquakes that are long overdue, many Christian leaders believe we are on the verge of another great awakening. They point to the fact that there have been five great awakenings throughout the history of the United States, beginning in 1740, 1792, 1830, 1858 and 1905. Each time these spiritual awakenings hit, the Holy Spirit brought revival to the church, an awakening among the unchurched and social reform to society.

But the sixth great awakening is long overdue. "Many of you who are alive today will live to see the great revival," shares C. Peter Wagner. "This is the spiritual awakening we and our parents have been praying for."

A World Still to Be Born

What can Renewal 2000 mega-images offer the bimillennial era as we seek to commemorate Jesus?

The strength of Renewal 2000 mega-images is that they call us to prayer and to nurture our private lives. They remind us the power of the Holy Spirit can enter our lives and enlarge the human spirit.

The weakness of Renewal 2000 can come when we try to emulate the past in the belief that if we could recover the moral meaning of America, then we would again be a great nation.

As mission leader Steve Hawthorne says, "It's not just revival—getting back to where we have been—but His *arrival*, welcoming the visitation of Christ at the break of a new day."

Is Something More Needed?

We have looked at four existing A.D. 2000 mega-images: Threshold 2000, Trends 2000, Agenda 2000, and Renewal 2000. Each of these represent an approach to how we have, up until now, looked toward the year 2000.[11] Is something more needed?

Could an A.D. 2000 mega-image be found to introduce and undergird the bimillennial era in such a way, that it would take our society beyond the bitterness of the present cultural wars?

A new mega-image would integrate, elaborate and amplify these previous four images into a "single great idea that can be easily grasped and simply shared."

When shared, a new A.D. 2000 mega-image, like a stone thrown into a pond, would send imaginative possibilities that ripple to the shores of our social boundaries.

If it was powerful, it would provoke cracks in our preconceptions, shift our misperceptions and help us live out a new vision together in a new world.

I consider the fifth mega-image, Jubilee 2000, to have the greatest potential to define and develop the bimillennial era. After all, Jesus used it himself.

*Proclaim liberty throughout all the
land unto all the inhabitants thereof.*
—*Leviticus 25:10, KJV*

6

We Are the
Jubilee Generation

The Liberty Bell is one of our world's most treasured relics
of independence. Its inscription is from the Bible, "Proclaim
liberty throughout all the land unto all the inhabitants
thereof." It was rung in 1776 to announce that a new era had
begun through the American Declaration of Independence.

On each successive anniversary, it was rung outside
Independence Hall in Philadelphia. Finally, in 1835, it broke
while tolling, leaving a famous crack up its middle. Even though
it rings no more, the Liberty Bell stands as a universal symbol
of freedom.

In ancient times, the law of Moses called for a year of liberty
every 50 years. You can read about it in Leviticus 25. Instead
of ringing a cast-iron bell, the Year of Jubilee was inaugurated
by the blowing of a great ram's horn trumpet (or jubal)
throughout the land. Thus began a year-long festival, marked
by canceling outstanding debts, returning land to original
owners and freeing indentured servants.

During this Sabbath of sabbath years, fields were not sowed,
nor vines pruned. This was meant to be a holy year marked by

75

reconciliation among families and communities. The Year of Jubilee gave a new lease on life to everyone.

I believe the year 2000 will be experienced as a once-in-a-lifetime Year of Jubilee. Jubilee 2000 is the most powerful image we could use to talk about the bimillennial of Jesus.

The Jubilee Edict

While no longer a social proposal as it was in ancient times, the Year of Jubilee nevertheless still stirs the imagination.[1]

In the case of Israel, it is uncertain whether the prescriptions of the Jubilee year were ever followed. What was meant to restore the inheritance of the fathers to each generation was neglected.

Almost a millennium passed before a generation in Israel had anything comparable to a jubilee experience. In 536 B.C., the ruler of the Persian empire, Cyrus the Great, was moved to release the people of Israel who had lived in exile for 70 years.

Two hundred years earlier, Isaiah prophesied that Cyrus would be God's chosen instrument to liberate the Jewish exiles. Tradition tells us that Cyrus was shown these prophesies in Isaiah 42, where God called him by name.

Later, using jubilee imagery, Isaiah captures this royal edict of release in chapter 61:1-4.

> The Spirit of the Sovereign Lord is on me,
> because the Lord has anointed me
> to preach good news to the poor.
> He has sent me to bind up the brokenhearted,
> to proclaim freedom for the captives
> and release from darksss for the prisoners,
> to proclaim the year of the Lord's favor
> and the day of vengeance of our God,
> to comfort all who mourn,
> and provide for those who grieve in Zion—
> to bestow on them a crown of beauty, instead of ashes,
> the oil of gladness instead of mourning,
> and a garment of praise instead of a spirit of despair.

Rather than the end of a 49-year cycle, Isaiah saw jubilee coming to the people of God when they most needed it. It would release them from slavery, bring them back into the land and restore their fortunes.

This would happen when a new regime came to power. The jubilee generation of Zerubbabel, Ezra, Nehemiah, Haggai and Zechariah did return and rebuild Jerusalem. Yet all of what a jubilee could bring would not be experienced until the anointed one came.

Jesus Is Our Jubilee

As a greater Cyrus, Jesus saw Himself as God's royal messenger of release. His coming opened a jubilee era of liberty for all humanity.

As Jesus announced His ministry in Nazareth, He applied the jubilee passage of Isaiah to the inauguration of God's reign (Luke 4:18-19), and later noted His healing ministry was evidence of its commencement (Matthew 11:2-6).

When Jesus ate with the elites of His day, He invited them to offer a jubilee experience to those the system had trodden down (Luke 14:12-14). His parables of banquet stories share how, in God's great feast, hunger and sadness are replaced by plenty and rejoicing (Luke 14:15-24).

In Jesus' jubilee, those ordinarily denied access to human occasions of celebration enjoy the blessings of society. The castaways are brought aboard. The lost sheep, the lost coin and the lost son are found.

What once was just a fifty-year event, or the moment of release of a people held captive, has become a perpetual jubilee. Through the cross of Christ, what was once released in a "year of redemption" has become available in an epoch without end.

As Gino Henriques of Evangelization 2000 says, "Through Jesus, we are always in the jubilee now. Every year is 'the year of the Lord's favor,' full of grace and forgiveness."

The Gregorian calendar gives testimony to the notion of this "acceptable time" tradition. Before each year we use the notation, A.D., or *Anno Domini*. A.D. 1995 stands for *Anno Domini*—the Year of Our Lord 1995.

Every year is the year of the Lord's favor. It takes an extraordinary year like 2000 to convince us that every year, every week, every day is the Lord's day and pregnant with meaning and possibilities.

You can almost hear the apostle Paul say, "It has been 1995 years since the jubilee of Jesus. But this year, this week, this day is still the acceptable time, the year of God's favor. Don't miss it." (cf. 2 Corinthians 6:1-2).

Open the Door of Jubilee

Like the ancient jubilee of Moses, the jubilee of Jesus suggests that each generation must respond to God's decree of liberty. This act of celebrating the grace of Christ and His redemptive work has not been lost on successive generations.

In A.D. 1300, Pope Boniface VIII, without any precedents, instituted a tradition within the Roman Catholic Church of celebrating every 100 years as a Holy Year of Jubilee. From all over Europe, pilgrims streamed to Rome to experience forgiveness and spiritual renewal.

"It was a wonderful spectacle," wrote Giovanni Villani, Florentine merchant and chronicler, "There were continually upwards of 100,000 pilgrims in the city, without counting those that each day came and went." Boniface's Jubilee year was "a centennial celebration of a new age that would begin with the clean slate of a year of absolution."[2]

Fifty years later a delegation came to Pope Clement to ask for a reduction of the Jubilee interval from one hundred years to fifty. They were desirous that their generation might experience the blessings of a Holy Year.

They reported that on the night before their audience with the pope "there appeared to us a vision of a certain venerable personage bearing two keys in his hand, who addressed to us the following words, 'Open the door, and from it send forth a fire by which the whole world may be warmed and enlightened.'" It is reported that the pope was so moved by their experience that he declared A.D. 1350 as a Holy Year.

A tradition developed that the Jubilee year began on Christmas Eve with the opening of a sealed golden door in St. Peter's Basilica. It affirmed that as the pope struck the holy door with a golden hammer, living streams of grace and pardon from Christ, the rock, were released. The inheritance of the fathers were restored to the sons.

Our Rendezvous With Destiny

Each generation seems to have it's own "rendezvous with destiny," as President Franklin Roosevelt once said. In hindsight, it seems his generation was called on to pull down the idols of fascism and communism so the world would be safe for democracy. What will be the rendezvous with destiny for our generation?

No one can be sure, but we may well be called upon to preserve the soul of Western civilization at a time when modern man increasingly rejects and despises the inheritance it has brought him.

In speaking about these cultural elites who despise the past, commentator Chuck Colson writes:

> And so, in the guise of pluralism and tolerance, they have set about to exile religion from our common life. They use the power of media and the law like steel wool to scrub public debates and public places bare of religious ideas and symbols. But what is left is sterile and featureless and cold.
>
> These elites seek freedom without self restraint, liberty without standards.
>
> The media celebrate sex without responsibility, and we are horrified by sexual plagues.

... A generation of cultural leaders want to live off the
spiritual capital of its inheritance, while denigrating
the ideals of its ancestors. It squanders a treasure it no
longer values. It celebrates its liberation when it
should be trembling for its future . . .

Disdaining the past and its values, we flee the judgment
of the dead. We tear down memory's monuments—
removing every guidepost and landmark—and wander
in unfamiliar country. But it is a sterile wasteland in
which men and women are left with carefully furnished
lives and utterly barren souls.

And so, paradoxically, at the very moment much of the
rest of the world seems to be reaching out for western
liberal ideas, the West itself, beguiled by myths of
modernity, is undermining the foundation of those
ideas.[3]

The Jubilee year of 2000 could not have come at a more
appropriate time. The civilization which began with the birth
of Jesus will encounter its spiritual roots on the occasion of the
bimillennial.

The season we are entering now is a *kairos* moment. It will
be super-charged with meaning due to the past and future. If
we respond to this epoch-making period it will surely be a
God-graced season. We dare not let it pass by unnoticed. It may
not come again.

Let the Jubilee Generation Arise

It is in this context I often share with groups that we are the
jubilee generation.

The past 25 years have witnessed a proliferation of generational terms. A whole new lexicon of terms have emerged such
as "generation gap," "Baby-boomers," and more recently
"Generation X," a more cynical younger twenty-something
crowd which is tired of generational scams.

By generation, I mean something larger than a single age group. It includes that, but it is much more. I see a generation as a group of people who live through the same epoch-making events of world history.

If we take a generation to be 40 years, and its been 2,000 years since Christ, that would mean that we are the 50th generation. In the Bible the year 50 is the Jubilee.

As the 50th generation since the birth of Christ, we are uniquely called to value, appreciate and celebrate the treasures of Christ in light of *Anno Domini* 2000. As we partake of this season of commemoration of Christ, we should ask God for a new lease on life, filled with more meaning and joy.

Celebrate the Celebrity

People can often have misconceptions when we talk about celebration. In the spring of 1992, I attended a New Life 2000 retreat of leaders at Arrowhead Springs, in San Bernardino, Calif. The first night, I had a memorable conversation with a Bible Society leader.

After introducing myself as the director of Celebration 2000—a consulting group for bimillennial initiatives, he launched into a monologue. "That's the problem with people today. They are so into celebrating themselves they are spoiled for anything else," he barked. "What about evangelism?"

Like many people, the first thought this leader had when he heard of Jubilee 2000 was partying. Our generation has never needed a reason to party, we just party to have a good time!

This is true for our secular celebrations, but the original sense of "celebrate" or "celebration" carried sacred connotations. The Oxford English Dictionary defines "celebrate" in these ways:
1. To perform publicly and in due form a religious ceremony.
2. To consecrate by religious rites.
3. To observe with solemn rites; to honor with religious ceremonies, festivities, or other observances.

4. To make publicly known, proclaim, publish abroad.
5. To speak the praises of, extol, publish the fame of.

In other words, celebrants at a celebration never celebrate themselves, but rather the celebrity. The celebrity, the star of 2000, will be Jesus.

Our culture responds well to celebrities. Whether it's sports stars like Michael Jordan, royalty like Lady Di or military heroes like Norman Swartzkopf, we shower them with admiration, adoration and affection. We seek to bask in their glory.

As worship teacher Judson Cornwall says, "We know quite well how to respond to a celebrity—unless that celebrity happens to be God, and then we respond as though we were attending a funeral."

Celebration in the original sense was never a memorial to the dead, but a celebration of the living God. The Jubilee was intended to be a year-long festival of the grace of God and the restoration of a lost inheritance to a new generation.

It was possible then, even as it is today, to get so caught up in the festivities as to forget the reason for celebration. If we are to be worthy of being called the "jubilee generation," we must not let this happen. We must celebrate the celebrity, not the celebration.

Starting Over at Year Zero

We must not forget who we are, and from where we have come. I often say that the prelude to the bimillennial era began in 1989, with a jubilee experience for people that had been captive under totalitarian regimes.

One observer said the ousting of the communist party took roughly ten years in Poland, ten months in Hungary, ten weeks in East Germany, ten days in Czechoslovakia and ten hours in Romania.

Vaclav Havel, the playwright who became Czechoslovakia's president, was asked how he felt about the theatrics begun in

1989. With unrehearsed elegance he replied, "It was a drama so thrilling and tragic and absurd that no earthling could have written it."

Then in August 1991, the tables were quickly turned on a gang of Kremlin hardliners, as Boris Yeltsin stood defiantly atop a rebel tank and thousands of citizens rallied to his defense. Within hours the hand of God released a people held in captivity for 70 years. Surely this was one of history's defining moments.

Spontaneous celebrations erupted everywhere. A Year of Jubilee had come. *Time* magazine ran a story entitled, "Standing at Year Zero." The Eastern Bloc's calendar was now pointed away from the old totalitarian regimes, whether czarist or communist. The odometer of history was reset. The challenge before them was to build a new order based on liberty, equality and justice.

The Jubilee Principle

The '60s were a time of political freedom for many colonial nations. Yet political freedom still left many Third World countries in economic bondage.

For years Martin Dent, economics professor at Keele University in England, wrestled with the problem of how Third World nations might compete on a level playing field in our global economy. Due to wild price swings for cash crops in the world commodity markets, many poorer nations were left crippled with the burden of unpayable debt.

He asked himself, how could this be corrected, since the general principle on which commercial life depends, is that debts must be repaid. He finally saw this could only be done by the jubilee principle of associating the debt remission with a special acceptable year which would not reoccur for a considerable time.

In 1989, Dent launched a "Jubilee 2000" campaign to call upon governments and banks to negotiate the cancellation of the backlogged debts of the world's poorest nations by 2000. In his discussions with governments around the world, he explains the roots of the jubilee principle from the Bible.

So They Might Worship Me

The Jubilee year of 2000 should be something far more than just an economic leveling program. At its essence, jubilee is a call to come into the presence of God and celebrate His greatness. When God instructed Moses to tell the Pharaoh of Egypt, "Let my people go!" it was "so they may worship me" (Exodus 4:22).

In his insightful book, *The Kingdom of God Is a Party*, Tony Campolo talks about how he had gotten it all wrong when it came to setting aside 10 percent of our earnings for God. Before reading Deuteronomy 14:22-29, he thought the tithe collected in Israel was for the work of God (i.e. the ministries of the church). But as he re-read this passage, Campolo discovered the tithe was not for that at all. It was for celebration!

Campolo writes, "Once a year . . . all the people of God were to bring one-tenth of all their earnings to the temple in Jerusalem ... And it was not used for mission work. It was not used for charity. It was not even to be used to build an education annex onto the temple. It was to be used on a gigantic party."[4]

The annual calendar of Israel was built around three major festivals: Passover, Pentecost and Tabernacles. These celebrations in Jerusalem were anything but boring. There was dancing, singing and exuberant celebration before the living God.

The Year of Jubilee encompassed these three festivals, only raised to a higher power. The clear call of God across the millennia is that we are invited to come into His presence and feast on Him.

On the last and greatest day of the Feast of Tabernacles, Jesus "stood and said in a loud voice, 'If anyone is thirsty, let him come to me and drink'" (John 7:37). Then as well as today, Jesus calls us to experience His jubilee.

Jubilee 2000

Jubilee remains the most exact biblical and contemporary metaphor for what the year 2000 ought to mean to the world. We still use the word "jubilee" to designate the celebration of special anniversaries, such as a silver jubilee, a 25th wedding anniversary, or a golden jubilee, the 50th.

Like the biblical Jubilee year, the coming bimillennial should be a time of reconciliation and celebration before God. This ordinary year, A.D. 2000, needs to be celebrated in an extraordinary way, particularly in light of Jesus' 2,000th birthday.

It's time again to ring the freedom bell. It's time to blow the ancient trumpet. It's time to be reconciled to our spiritual roots. Heaven is calling us to come and worship. We are the jubilee generation and a Year of Jubilee is at hand.

*The year 2000 will open the floodgates
of commemorative consciousness.*
—William Johnston

7

The Anniversary Attraction

Saints and sinners fascinate us, even long after their time. In 1988, British tabloids celebrated the centennial of Jack the Ripper, London's notorious serial killer. Between July and November of that year, his century-old slayings on London's East End received much fanfare.

Anniversaries attract us. In some strange fashion, they allow us to relive history. Whether a landmark event, an invention, or birth or death of a famous person, it is the 10th, 20th, 40th, 50th, or 100th anniversary that we usually commemorate.

Last year we celebrated the centennial of the ferris wheel, the zipper and the X-ray machine. Also commemorated was the 30th anniversary of the death of Marilyn Monroe and the 30th anniversary of Martin Luther King, Jr.'s famous civil rights march on Washington, D.C.

This year we commemorate the 50th anniversary of D-Day at Normandy. Next year we celebrate the 50th birthday of the United Nations. In 1996, we mark the centennial of the Nobel Peace Prize, and the modern Olympic Games.

In the past twenty years, the modern age of anniversaries

has spawned huge commemorative, heritage and travel industries. Already this mega-anniversary complex has turned its eyes on the year 2000. This anniversary will differ from others in that the turn of the calendar touches all humanity.

The world has never celebrated a centennial or millennial together, much less a bimillennial.

Many groups see celebration 2000 more from the vantage point of Times Square than Bethlehem's manger square. Unaware that A.D. 2000 will be the most remarkable Christmas in 2,000 years, they only look upon it as the biggest New Year's in a 1,000 years.[1]

Meet Me by the Great Pyramid!

One group which is making big plans for December 31, 1999 is The Millennium Society. It was founded in 1979 by a handful of Yale students. One afternoon over brunch, Ed McNally and his friends mused what it would be like to have their 20th class reunion in 1999. Refusing to accept the popular notion that the world would soon be destroyed by nuclear war, McNally and friends formed an organization that would optimistically welcome the new millennium.

Already The Millennium Society has reserved the Great Pyramid of Cheops near Cairo, Egypt, on December 31, 1999, for three thousand optimists to celebrate the history of civilization, and to look ahead to progress in the third millennium.

The Queen Elizabeth II, also reserved, will set sail from New York harbor for a ten-day cruise to this last remaining Wonder of the World in time to ring in 2000. Among those invited on the millennial cruise are Steven Speilberg, Corazón Aquino, Bill Clinton, Michael Jackson, and Deng Xiaoping. Comedian George Burns, who will be 103 by then, is also invited to attend the black-tie affair—with a date.

Besides the Great Pyramid party, McNally and associates have celebrations planned in each of the twenty-four times zones on December 31, 1999. So, as the arrival of the year 2000 crosses the international date line in New Zealand and sweeps across this planet, celebrants will be at the Great Wall of China, the Taj Mahal, the Acropolis, the Eiffel Tower, Stonehenge, Times Square and the Golden Gate Bridge (and that is the short list!).

Do the Maximum for the Millennium

Besides college students, the year 2000 has also been grist for magazine columnists up and down the land. *New York Times* humorist, Lewis Grossberger, playfully suggests that Americans must celebrate the year 2000 with all the grandiosity, excess and overkill that it can muster. "We'll need the greatest procession of tall ships ever. I propose manning them with short sailors, to make them seem even taller."

Grossberger further suggests that we need to work on commercial tie-ins for the year 2000—like which brand of diet soda, light beer or wine cooler will be the official drink of the millennium? After all, as Grossberger reminds us, "America must do more than the minimum on the millennium."

Make Those Reservations Early!

For Edward Woodyard, a free-lance writer from Armonk, N.Y., it pays to plan ahead. In the fall of 1983, Woodyard was listening to the sounds of the high school band rehearse down the street. Musing on how time flies, he commented to his brother-in-law how soon there would be a class of 2000.

Then it hit him, "God, 2000 is going to be some New Year's Eve." Woodyard decided he better hurry up and make his hotel reservations at Times Square if he wanted to see the zeroes on history's odometer turn over.

The following Monday he called the Mariott Hotel chain, owners of the still unbuilt Times Square hotel, to make his reservation for December 31, 1999. They realized the publicity potential of having the first person make a millennial hotel reservation—and gave Woodyard a free four-bedroom suite overlooking Times Square. To announce this year 2000 reservation, the Mariott threw a press conference on December 28, 1983. The place was mobbed. The story hit the newspapers and went on the wires. CNN ran a piece on it and Johnny Carson squeezed a line out of it.

A Trivia 2000 Book

New Yorkers are so serious about their millennium's eve parties they write trivia books on it. In 1991, Bantam Doubleday Dell released *The Millennium Book* by Gail & Dan Collins, two New York journalists.[2]

This book is perfect for any millennial party animal. Through humorous top ten lists, critics share the best or worse of the last millennium, including the top ten tunes, the ten best parties, the ten worst natural disasters and the ten worst meals, including Spam.

Also reviewed are the prophets whose forecasts for the year 2000 will launch a thousand talk show discussions, including Nostradamus, Jean Dixon and St. Malachy.

A World Thanksgiving Year

Not everyone in New York is looking to commercialize the bimillennial. Leaders at the United Nations have been talking about celebrating the year 2000 as a world Thanksgiving year since the late '70s.

UN watchers predict that after the United Nations celebrates its own 50th jubilee in 1995, it will officially announce this year 2000 jubilee for humanity. A former assistant secretary-general of the UN has written a novel to suggest how the UN ought to prepare for this coming International Year of Thanksgiving.

Robert Muller's book, *The First Lady of the World* begins in 1992 with the hypothetical inauguration of the first woman secretary-general. She is an Indian diplomat named Lakshmi Narayan. Inspired by a wise Frenchman, she becomes an advocate for worldwide celebrations of the year 2000 preceded by unparalleled thinking, inspiration, and planning for the achievement of a peaceful and happy human society on earth.

By 1996, the arms race ends, and a World Peace Service is created to allow young people to do world service in poor countries, in lieu of abolished military service. In 1998, a World Constitutional Assembly is convened in Philadelphia and given till 1999 to come up with a World Constitution to fulfill the dreams of Simon Bolivar and George Washington.

A Bimillennial Scenario

The novel, *The First Lady of the World* reaches a crescendo in the bimillennium.

> The year 2000 was an incredible event. Ever since the UN General Assembly recommended to hold this world-wide celebration, ideas, visions, programs, projects, movements, institutions, awards and pub-licity campaigns for the year 2000 and the advent of the third millennium sprang up all over the world.

> It was a universal outbidding of enthusiasm, inspira-tion, imagination, discussions, and conferences on the expected new age. The UN received news of dozens of conferences being held to contribute to the year. Every nation established a national committee for the preparation and celebration of the bimillennium.

> Every TV network on earth commissioned programs reviewing how the world had changed since the year 1000 or the beginning of the century and what humanity could dream for the next millennium. Books were published showing the state of the world and of humanity 3,000, 2,000, 1,000 years before Christ, in the years 1, 1000 and 2000.

> Each Earth Day was bigger than the preceding. Ecologists and the youth of the sixties saw the triumph

of many of their ideas. The Catholics started an evangelization 2000 movement. All religions cooperated in an ecumenic council for the year 2000.

The Pope presented his views on a third, spiritual millennium to the 1994 UN General Assembly, during the International Year of the Family. The whole UN and its agencies were busy updating and putting together their plans 2000 and beyond.

School children had contests on their views of the year 2000 and the next millennium. Universities and research institutes were overflowing with theses and books on the third millennium in all realms of science, technology, social, political, ethical, moral, philosophical and spiritual concerns.

It was simply unbelievable.

The sports joined in and organized special events and competitions in 2000. The arts flourished with innumerable year 2000 productions, rediscovering the beauty and harmony all around us, repeating the miracle of the Italian Renaissance after the bewildered, chaotic, scared Middle Ages.

Every conceivable celebration took place in the world, in capitals, in cities, in villages, in churches, in hamlets, in families. The grand opening of the world celebration took place on New Years' eve, 31 December 1999. Festivities and world prayers were held all over the planet, re-transmitted by all television networks.

Never had such a thing happened in the entire human history.[3]

Stealing Our Thunder?

The bimillennium will undoubtedly attract unprecedented attention, culminating in 1999, 2000 and 2001 with extravaganzas which will unite the world as never before.

How should we feel about this? In response to these millennium theme trips and parties being planned, one religious leader told me, "The year 2000 is a Christian occasion. They have no right to steal our thunder!" Could this assertion be true?

◆ Will the biggest New Year's Eve in a 1,000 years be celebrated with such overkill and excess that it will preempt the celebration of the most sacred Christmas in 2,000 years?

◆ Will humanity miss "the reason for the season" if the year 2000 is celebrated as a world Thanksgiving year?

◆ Is the world fast developing a way to celebrate the year 2000 that might totally overlook history's most influential person—Jesus Christ?

◆ Is the year 2000 exclusively a Christian anniversary?

I would answer "no" to each of these questions. The world's anniversary attraction to 2000 should not be interpreted as a countercommemoration of Jesus' bimillennial.

There are historical reasons why the year 2000 will bring such a mix of sacred and secular celebrations.

The Christian Calendar
The reason why some will celebrate the year 2000 in a secular way, and others in a sacred manner, is that our civil calendar was derived from the Christian calendar.

The year 2000, therefore, carries both secular and sacred connotations. It is both C.E. 2000 and A.D. 2000, both Common Era and *Anno Domini* (the Year of Our Lord).

Before civilization emerged, people lived season to season, year to year, and gave little thought to historical eras. Calendars were established on national or religious beginnings.

The Hebrew calendar started counting from creation, a moment supposed to be 3,760 years before the Christian era.

The Romans counted their calendar from the mythical birth of Rome in a year we designate as 753 B.C.

Every succeeding centennial was a celebration of the continuity and achievements of the Roman era. In A.D. 247, Emperor Philip Arabian celebrated the 1,000th anniversary of the Roman era.

The reference event for the Christian calendar was the birth of Christ in A.D. 1, as calculated by Dionysius Exiguus in A.D. 525. In 1582, Pope Gregory XIII fine-tuned the Christian calendar by revising the Julian calendar's reckoning of leap years. Even so, the Gregorian calendar or New Style calendar, remained exclusively European for almost 200 years. It was not until 1752 that England and the American colonies fully accepted it. Japan adopted it in 1873, followed by Egypt in 1875.

Only after the Chinese and Russian revolutions of this century did the whole world begin using the same calendar. By the end of World War II the Gregorian calendar took a predominant role among world calendars and its widespread use regulated trade, travel and intergovernmental affairs.

Due to these developments, the year 2000 will be the first time in history that the whole world has celebrated a centennial, a millennial, or much less a bimillennial together.

The Gregorian calendar is now called the common calendar, due to its universal application.

Although technically the common calendar counts from the birth of Christ, the annotations C.E. are not meant to refer to the Christian era. The common civil calendar is a secular abstraction meant to function without reference to a single culture or starting point.

The Rise of Secular Anniversaries

Originally, the anniversary attraction was created by the historic churches through the liturgical calendar. Its purpose was to celebrate the life of Christ and the history of the church each year through designated holy days.

By the sixth century, the liturgical calendar was fully developed. The church year celebrated Christmas, preceded by a season of Advent, then Easter, preceded by a time of penitence and, finally, Pentecost, followed by a season where the acts of the apostles were celebrated. Many saints' days, as well, were recognized and celebrated on the annual cycle.

Before 1700, very few secular anniversaries in Europe were celebrated. Up until that time, only the birthdays of lords and ladies had been important enough to warrant celebration. Commoners rarely kept the dates of their birth, much less celebrated them.

National celebrations were practically unknown until the French Revolution commemorated its first anniversary in 1793. This same need to articulate a national identity prompted the United States to celebrate July 4th as Independence Day.

Rather than jettison the Christian calendar, what modern society has done is secularize it, by replacing Christian anniversaries with cultural or civic ones. Instead of holy days, we now have holidays.

In America we celebrate New Year's Day, Valentine's Day, President's Day, Memorial Day, Mother's Day, Father's Day, Independence Day, Labor Day and Halloween.

Instead of a Sabbath, we have the "weekend" which extends from Friday (or T.G.I.F.) to Monday night football. Leisure through entertainment or recreation has become the reward for labor.

The Agenda Setters

Gone are the days when the church alone could set the anniversary agenda for society.

In addition to the state and media, we have the heritage, travel and sports industries promoting their own brand of anniversaries, each worshiping their own images and achievements. All these institutions will gear up for the bimillennial.

Perhaps we should adopt the attitude of William Booth, founder of the Salvation Army, when he asked, "Why should the devil have all the good tunes?"

In the 1870s, his combination of religious lyrics with stirring bar music took hope and redemption to a whole new generation in London. At the time he was ridiculed and criticized, but later gained the highest respect. If we are to impact our society during bimillennial era, we will need to take a lesson from Booth.

Taking Our Cities to God

Several years ago, John Dawson wrote a very original book entitled *Taking Our Cities for God*.[4] In it he described how to study and grasp your city's spiritual history, and, through prayer and positive action, break the "strongholds" that keep people captive. Networks of church leaders in various cities emerged across denominational lines to spiritually map their city and engage in spiritual warfare.

This spiritual warfare movement has been greatly needed, and has brought much reconciliation between groups. I see this movement as only a forerunner of the greater work of God in our cities as we approach the bimillennial. In contrast to spiritual warfare, I call it "spiritual procession." Rather than take our cities *for* God, the emphasis is taking our cities *to* God.

As we prepare to celebrate Jesus' bimillennial in the context of the anniversary attraction, here are three steps to spiritual procession:

Recover the meaning of celebration.

Two years ago I had a memorable visit with Dr. Richard Halverson, chaplain to the United States Senate. In response to my vision for celebration 2000 he said, "This is near to the heart of God. If you are doing this to impress the world, forget it. Don't let it become a gimmick." That was good advice then and now.

The bimillennial must first and foremost be something of great value to God. We are on the wrong track if we aim to impress the world through our celebrations of Jesus' bimillennial. As the church in the city, we need to recover a theology of celebration.

The celebration of the bimillennial needs to go far beyond commemorating the life and legacy of Jesus to releasing extraordinary movements of praise and worship of Christ, who has the name above all names.

The obvious starting place to recover the meaning of celebration is the Old Testament. Here worship is built around festivals, feasts and fellowship on sacred days. At least three times a year the people of Israel would go up to Jerusalem to delight in God's presence.

The next time you look at a concordance, or bring up a computer Bible program, do a word study on feasts, festivals, sabbath, sacred assemblies, jubilee, worship, offerings, temple, praise, priests or processions. What do these passages say about celebrating the living God on special occasions?

Turning to the New Testament, the spotlight shifts to Jesus. The books of Colossians and Hebrews reminds us that He is exalted to the throne of God, where we have full access. The book of Revelation is full of celebration scenes of heavenly worship.

On the basis of your theology of celebration, what would it look like for the churches in your city to celebrate Jesus' bimillennial together as we approach the year 2000?

Discover the significance of anniversaries.

Having recovered the meaning of biblical celebration, you should discover the significance of anniversaries.

Sacred and secular anniversaries have a lot more in common than meets the eye. One may use ritual or liturgy, the other pageantry or ceremony. While there is no academic study of mega-anniversaries, one starting point in understanding their significance is your public library. Check the card catalogue under a variety of subject headings including anniversaries, bicentennial or centennial celebrations, holidays and special occasions, feasts and festivals, rites and rituals, myths and customs, work and play, and symbol theory.

One of Canada's leading celebrants is Peter Aykroyd. His son is also a celebrity—Dan Aykroyd of Blues Brothers fame! When Canada celebrated its centennial in 1967, it turned to Peter Aykroyd to manage public relations.

In his recent book *The Anniversary Compulsion*, Peter Aykroyd shares how the Centennial Commission worked for seven years to refine the concept, structure, process and procedures of the Canadian centennial.

What was missing, Aykroyd felt, was any comprehensive understanding of what a mega-anniversary ought to mean to a community, city or nation.

To help anniversary planners develop successful celebrations, Aykroyd offers ten anniversary axioms.[5] In summary fashion they are:

1. Reinforce our unique identity.
2. Restate our shared history and achievement.
3. Accentuate unifying elements: symbols, songs, etc.
4. Aggressively oppose destructive forces.
5. Focus on the future voyage to inspire confidence.
6. Encourage personal and community involvement.
7. Build monuments and memorials.
8. Give gifts that keep on giving.
9. Set up performances, public events and shared experiences.
10. Release the anniversary spirit through fun, using both ceremony and celebration.

The Aykroyd axioms are indispensable guidelines for bimillennial celebrations.

Uncover the redemptive gift of your city.

The third step to spiritual procession in light of the bimillennial is to ask, "What is my city's redemptive gift and how is this affirmed and shared with others through celebration?" A look at churches, non-profit groups and annual festivals in your community will reveal some clues.

In 1978, Olgy and I moved to Pasadena, Calif., which became our home for 14 years. I will never forget New Year's Day in 1980 when I saw my first Rose Parade live. We arrived at Colorado Boulevard about 1 a.m., and the New Year's Eve celebrations were still going strong.

We spent the night in sleeping bags on the sidewalk, saving our second row seats. The parade started the next morning at 9 a.m. Along with a million others, we took in the smells, sights and sounds of America's premier holiday parade.

As the years passed by, I began to realize how much the Rose Parade expressed the identity of old Pasadena. The Rose Parade, with its floats, beauty queens and grand marshals, was really a mega-statement of civic pride in the beauty and order of life. Life was full of fragrance for those who stopped to smell the roses.

John Dawson says each city embodies a central dream, personality, or God-given "redemptive gift." As a community lives in righteousness, it fulfills its redemptive purpose. What is the redemptive gift of your city? How is that gift affirmed and shared with others through celebration?

You might find some clues through a visit to your local Convention and Visitor's Bureau. Ask for a list of annual festivals.

In 1992, we moved to Colorado Springs, Colo. As I read the local newspaper every day that first year, I made it a point to clip every article on annual city festivals, from the Festival of Learning to the Balloon Classic. By the end of my first year, I had an inch thick file with newspaper clippings and a better idea of the redemptive gift of my city.

There is something about the "purple mountains' majesty" of Colorado Springs that rekindles the spirit, and releases your soul to mount up to new heights. Uncovering your city's redemptive gift can go far beyond identifying its annual festivals.

Another window on the redemptive gift of your city would be to make a list of the top ten churches in your community and look at their gifts or charismas. What are they known for? Is it worship, service or fellowship? How do the churches, or your church in particular, contribute to the redemptive gift of your city?

A study of the leading non-profit groups in your city can also be helpful. I was surprised to learn that non-profits, whether religious, human service, cultural or sports make up more than 8 percent of the economy of Colorado Springs.

Only one-fifth of these 500 groups are related to the church in any way. All of them, however, contribute to a higher quality of life in our city.

In my research, I found myself using what my friend, Steve Vannoy, calls the FAC tool.

◆ Find

◆ Acknowledge

◆ Celebrate

When I find a festival, church or public benefit group that is really shaping my city's redemptive identity, I acknowledge it and celebrate its presence.

As we prepare for Jesus' bimillennial, I believe this is one way we can move in priestly roles to call forth those cultural treasures that presently lie hidden in our midst.

Man is the caretaker
and cantor of the universe.
—Rabbi Abraham Heschel

8

A Symphony of Praise

In seeking to describe the way that galaxies, stars, planets and all living things interact with one another, scientists are now saying that "celebration" might be the most appropriate expression. Everything about us seems absorbed in one grand cosmic symphony. Even the afflictions cannot diminish the songs that resonate throughout the natural world.[1]

I have a feeling that when God first created the world He did it through song. When He sang, "Let there be light," it was so. Then the light echoed back a refrain of praise, and God said, "It was good." God is not just the creator, but also the composer and conductor of the universe. It is to Him that the universe sings its song.

In honor of Jesus, the heavenly conductor may well compose a new "hymn of the universe" in time for the bimillennial.

The Hymn of the Universe
One of the most enduring hymns of all times has been St. Francis of Assisi's "Canticle of the Sun." Surely, this canticle must be one of those hymns of the universe. Its lead chorus is

"All praise be yours, my Lord, through all that you have made."
Next Francis sings, "All praise be yours, my Lord, through all
that you have made, and first my lord Brother Sun."

Each refrain that follows speaks of the praise brought to
Christ by "sister Moon," "brother Wind," or "sister Earth" to
name a few.

A couple of years ago, I was visiting my wife's family in
New Jersey and planned a day full of appointments at the
United Nations. I remember waking up that August morning
singing a song I hadn't sung for more than 15 years. It was
called, "Sing to God a Brand New Canticle." I thought nothing
of it at the time.

Later that day, I had lunch with Brother Kevin Smith, head
of the Franciscan mission to the United Nations. As we talked
about the bimillennial, and the unique role of Franciscans
worldwide in preparation for it, I shared with him my morning
experience.

He said, "Funny you should mention that, before you came
I felt that the 'Canticle of the Sun' would be one of our greatest
gifts to the celebrations of the year 2000."

I do not believe we will see the fullness of the bimillennial
era of Jesus unfold until we, like St. Francis, catch a vision for
praise and worship being brought unto Him.

The Rock at Rockville

This insight that the door to the bimillennial era of Jesus
might be unlocked through praise and worship first came to
me back in 1988. While working for the Lausanne movement,
I was asked to join a meeting in Rockville, Va., to help plan
what became GCOWE 2000, the historic "Global Consultation
on World Evangelization by AD 2000 and Beyond" just six
months later. We opened that evening on June 4th with a
landmark presentation on the "unfinished task" by mission
researcher David Barrett.

I returned to my room that night convinced that Barrett's
new study would set the agenda of the church as we approached

the year 2000. As I started to record this conviction in my journal, I was interrupted by God.

The Holy Spirit seemed to flood my soul lighting up the reality of Ephesians 2:21 which says, "In Him, the whole building is joined together and rises to be a holy temple in the Lord." I spent the next two hours worshipping God as I filled page upon page with spiritual reflections.

Up until that time, I had given little thought to what it meant to bring an offering into God's temple. Yet, that night it was as if the Lord said to me, "The real rock, the real building about to be built, will be into Christ as a holy temple. You will witness this movement of praise as you approach the year 2000." The conductor of the universe was about to compose something new in honor of His Son.

A New Orchestration

I believe a new work of God has begun deep within the heart of the church to focus us on Jesus as never before. Even now, this divine orchestration is hidden. What lies concealed will soon be revealed. An hour is coming when Christ will be all in our lives.

At the turn of the century, Ignace Paderewski was known as a world-class pianist, composer and patriot from Poland. The story is told of how a mother, who wanted to encourage her 7-year-old son in his lessons, took her boy to hear one of Paderewski's concerts.

Mother and son arrived at the concert early in order to find a good seat, but somehow her son slipped out of her sight. After looking in the lobby, she entered the auditorium. Standing in the back she saw her son was up on stage playing chop sticks!

You can imagine the embarrassment she felt. Some people where actually yelling, "Get that kid away from there." She made her way down to the front only to notice a man was sitting next to her son.

Unannounced by the program, Paderewski had come in 15 minutes early to warm up. With her son playing chop sticks at his side, Paderewski began to play the most magnificent accompanying piece. The mother could hear Paderewski saying to her son, "You're doing fine, don't stop now, keep playing chop sticks."

Now is not the time to grow weary or faint. God is about to play a magnificent symphony of praise in honor of His Son. He intends for us to be His instruments.

You may feel like you're playing mere child's games or chop sticks when you come before the presence of God in praise and prayer.

But you are never alone—the Father is always at your side. And the Holy Spirit is weaving your life into a heavenly harmony before the throne of God.

Concerts of Prayer

How will this symphony of praise be expressed as we approach the bimillennial? Some look for an unprecedented rising tide of prayer to swell up in our cities.

In 1988, David Bryant founded a ministry called Concerts of Prayer International (COPI) to strengthen what he saw as an emerging groundswell of prayer within cities for spiritual awakening and world evangelization.

Today COPI works with volunteers in hundreds of cities to convene large-scale prayer gatherings called Concerts of Prayer. What makes these gatherings so different?

Whether they meet in a city monthly or quarterly, Concerts of Prayer are different in make up. They gather a broader representation of people from various denominations, age groups and social settings. COPI compares these gatherings to musical concerts. Instead of musical instruments blending in some grand symphony, believers from various backgrounds blend their hearts, minds and voices in faith before the throne of God into one harmonious celebration.

Concerts of Prayer are also unique in their exclusive focus on Christ. Their prayer focus is twofold: (1) prayer for God to reveal to His Church the *fullness* of Christ as Lord in her midst, and (2) prayer for the resulting *fulfillment* of the purposes of God through the church among the nations.

COPI is just one part of an unprecedented modern prayer movement that researchers estimate to be 170 million and growing daily. Very soon, the prayer movement, with its 1,400 networks worldwide, will turn its eyes toward the Star of 2000.

We may see the bimillennial era of Jesus characterized by a crescendo of intercession coming from prayer concerts, prayer summits and solemn assemblies.

If this surge of prayer continues as we approach the bimillennial, Bryant believes the church may experience what the Puritans used to call "the manifest presence of Christ." In his latest book, Bryant writes, "This is Christ coming to His people in fullness, dwelling among them in fresh and powerful ways, revealing to us His glory, filling us with His wisdom, demonstrating to us His wonders and miracles, and calling us to go with Him as He seeks and saves the lost."[2]

Come Into His Presence

Another expression of spiritual procession is through praise and worship. The Lord may well use the bimillennial to bring back to Christ the glory which, during many centuries, has largely been turned aside to man.

In the past twenty years, millions of people have experienced a rebirth of worship in their lives and congregations. They have begun to understand that the Lord is the only audience, and we are called to give glory to His name.

For years, I was interested in the year 2000, but my real heart pilgrimage to the bimillennial, my spiritual procession to Christ, was transformed in January 1991 as a result of attending a worship symposium in my area. It opened a whole new world to me in personal praise and worship.

Later, that experience was deepened as we regularly attended a worship rally called Presencia. Once a month, 3,000 Hispanics would crowd into the Los Angeles College auditorium for three hours of worship. A spirit of joy filled that place as Christ was lifted up. This kind of city-wide praise gathering will most likely multiply during the bimillennial era.

I still sing a favorite song from those Presencia meetings called, "Estamos de Fiesta." It so captures what it means to be in procession to Jesus' jubilee. The translation loses a little in the process, but it goes something like this:

> We are going to a fiesta with Jesus,
> to the Father we want to go.
> Everyone is reunited at the table,
> and Jesus will now serve us.
> Our God is powerful! Our God is powerful!

Worship 2000

Through prayer, more often than not, we present our needs to God. Through praise we offer thanks for our blessings. Through worship we release our soul to magnify the greatness of God. This is why the Psalmist could sing:

> Shout for joy to the Lord, all the earth.
> Worship the Lord with gladness;
> come before him with joyful songs
> (Psalm 100:1-3).

If the only trumpet we blow during the bimillennial era is "come and worship Him" it will be enough.

Three years ago, I noticed a Worship 2000 conference was being held in Atlanta. Interested in the theme, I contacted Lamar Boschman, dean of the International Worship Leaders Institute, which sponsored the program. I asked, "Why did you call this conference 'Worship 2000' and how does this relate to the year 2000 being a holy year of Jubilee?" He told me the Worship 2000 focus came from the vision of stadiums full of people worshiping God as we approach the year 2000.

Believe me, the Father has already charged the angels of heaven to gather up from the East to the West one great offering of praise to present to our Lord on His 2,000th birthday.

The Temple of Living Stones

This calling to present unto God a gift of praise filled the hearts of first century Christians. The apostles taught that a house of God, a temple of worship, is being built for all nations.

Originally, the church was comprised of converted Jews. When great numbers of Gentiles started to turn to Christ, James, the brother of Jesus, saw this as fulfillment of prophecy.

During the first church council in Jerusalem, he quoted the prophet Amos: "After this I will return and rebuild David's fallen tent . . . that the remnant of men may seek the Lord, and all the Gentiles who bear my name . . . " (Acts 15:16-17).

A millennia earlier, King David sought to restore true worship of the living God. He appointed Levite musicians to serve God in worship day and night. James saw Jesus as the greater son of David, sent to erect "David's fallen tent."

The apostle Peter saw the church as a temple of living stones. He wrote: "As you come to him, the living Stone— rejected by men but chosen by God and precious to him—you also, like living stones, are being built into a spiritual house to be a holy priesthood, offering spiritual sacrifices acceptable to God through Jesus Christ" (1 Peter 2:4-5).

The apostle Paul saw himself as a temple builder, a stone gatherer among the Gentile nations. He saw his missionary work among the Gentiles as a "priestly service" so that they might become an offering acceptable to God.

He exhorted the Romans to be unified "so that with one heart and mouth" both Jews and Gentiles might together "glorify the God and Father of our Lord Jesus Christ" (Romans 15:6).

An Eternal Cathedral of Praise

We are so used to seeing history from a man-centered framework, we lose sight of the fact that all generations are coming before the throne of God with their gifts.

The author of Hebrews exhorted the early Christians to run their race knowing that they were surrounded by a cloud of witnesses who had gone before them. He concludes by saying:

> But you have come to Mount Zion,
> to the heavenly Jerusalem,
> the city of the living God.
> You have come to thousands upon thousands
> of angels in joyful assembly,
> to the church of the firstborn . . .
> You have come to God, the judge of all men,
> to the spirits of righteous men made perfect,
> to Jesus the mediator of a new covenant . . .
> (Hebrews 12:22-24).

What a vision for the year 2000 and beyond! Worship in the house of God is well underway. Offerings are pouring in day by day from among the nations. Our bimillennial celebrations of Christ are but a later, greater offering in this procession.

An eternal cathedral of praise is being erected in Christ, from the ruins of this world. This is the greatest reclamation project in the universe.

As we bring a gift of praise in honor of His Son, we become the building materials, those living stones fashioned together in Christ to be His eternal temple of worship to God. All of our efforts for the bimillennial need to be seen in this light.

As we approach 2000, we need to affirm that this spiritual building is growing across our world. A new symphony of praise is about to begin in honor of Jesus.

Perhaps when we begin this latest orchestration, the presence of God will fill the whole earth, just as it once filled the temple of old with glory.

*But thanks be to God, who always
leads us in Christ's triumphant train.
—the apostle Paul*

9

The March of
the Millennium

Several years ago Colleen McCullough, author of *The Thorn
Birds* brought out another spellbinding novel, *A Creed for the
Third Millennium*.[1] In it, McCullough weaves into a religious
story both emotional intensity and a powerful climax.

The story is set in 2033. A spreading ice age has forced
millions of people around the globe to migrate to southern
climates. Worldwide economies have collapsed. To ease the
population crunch, the United States has been forced to adhere
to a one-child policy. "Millennial neurosis," the loss of hope
in God or humanity, is epidemic.

Enter Dr. Joshua Christian, a clinical psychologist, who
offers a demoralized nation faith in his self-styled God.
Through the help of Dr. Judith Carriol, an ambitious senior
official in the department of environment, Dr. Christian rises
from obscurity to worldwide fame.

As the story progresses, his messianic complex is matched
only by Judith Carriol's ambition to control him. The climax
of this crusade comes through a cosmic walk-a-thon, called the
"March of the Millennium," led by the doctor himself, from

New York to Washington, D.C. Reaching out to the cold hands and despairing hearts of the American people, the personal magnetism of Dr. Christian transforms this final tour into an epic pilgrimage that touches and renews millions. As a result America awakens, and is on the move again at the dawn of the third millennium.

The March of the Century

The vision of masses on the move, marching through history, is a stirring one. We can remember much of this century through its marches. Hitler marched his troops by torchlight. Stalin marched his artillery through Red Square. Mao's Red Guard marched throughout China and ravaged a nation.

On the other hand, the 20th century has experienced many redemptive marches. In 1930, Gandhi led hundreds of followers on a 200-mile march to the sea. His nonviolent campaign won the respect of the world and gained independence from Britain.

In 1963, Martin Luther King, Jr. led a historic civil rights march to the Lincoln Memorial. It was inspiration—some say divine inspiration—that led King to put aside his prepared remarks that day and deliver his famous "I Have a Dream" speech.

> I say to you today, my friends, so even though we face the difficulties of today and tomorrow, I still have a dream. It is a dream deeply rooted in the American dream.
>
> I have a dream that one day this nation will rise up and live out the true meaning of its creed: 'We hold these truths to be self-evident: that all men are created equal.'
>
> I have a dream that one day on the red hills of Georgia the sons of former slaves and the sons of former slave owners will be able to sit down together at the table of brotherhood . . .

I have a dream that my four little children will one day
live in a nation where they will not be judged by the
color of their skin, but by the content of their
character.

I have a dream today!

Many believe this march and King's eloquent vision of
justice was a turning point which created the momentum in the
United States Congress to pass the 1964 Civil Rights Act.

A Greater March

Indeed, this century has seen some great marches. Yet these
marches pale in comparison to the true and greater march led
by Jesus. As a greater Moses, Jesus is leading a greater exodus
as we cross into the third millennium. I believe it rightfully
should be called, the "March of the Millennium."

This march of Jesus is old, yet new. It has swept through
space and time, enlisting many generations and encompassing
practically all nations. We may well see it swell in numbers as
we approach the bimillennial.

The biblical history of spiritual procession is a rich one. It
first surfaced in Genesis 35, when Jacob and his household
marched up to Bethel, "the house of God," and built an altar.[2]

Four hundred years later, Moses awoke the masses in Egypt,
only to have the Lord march the children of Israel out of captivity. This spiritual procession numbered in the millions as
they marched to Mt. Sinai, and into the promised land.

In 2 Samuel 6, David brought the ark of God back to Israel
with a great procession of singers and musicians, and conse-
crated Jerusalem as a capital city.

After the captivity in Babylon and Persia, Ezra and Nehemiah
lead a remnant back to Jerusalem in a joyful procession.

The Gospels describe Jesus' last year of ministry as a great
freedom march down through the Jordan valley, through
Jericho, and finally into Jerusalem with much public praise.
Throughout passion week, Jesus' march stirred the city of

Jerusalem. Many thought it was finished on Friday. But come Sunday, Jesus leapt from the grave, rose victorious over death and Satan, marched right past principalities, powers, thrones and dominions to the very throne of God!

Later, the apostle John gives us a glimpse of a "great multitude" gathered before "the throne and in front of the Lamb," having completed their march through history.

The term "Lamb," of course, is a symbolic title for Jesus, reminding us that His march took Him by way of the cross. John describes Jesus in this way: "For the Lamb at the center of the throne will be their shepherd; he will lead them to springs of living water" (Revelation 7:17). Speaking in categories which transcend space and time, Jesus is both the end and the leader of the "March of the Millennium."

This is why the apostle Paul could say, "But thanks be to God, who always leads us in triumphant procession in Christ" (2 Corinthians 2:14).

The people of the Roman empire were quite familiar with "triumphant processions." After a general won a great military campaign for the empire, he would march in "triumphant procession." With his army in front, followed by a defeated enemy in chains, the general would march into the city to receive his acclaim.

In a similar way, the Lord Jesus has won a great campaign, "having disarmed the powers and authorities, he made a public spectacle of them, triumphing over them by the cross" (Colossians 2:15).

His march then ended at the throne of God. He now reigns to receive acclaim and tribute from the nations, as Scripture says, "And all from Sheba will come, bearing gold and incense and proclaiming the praise of the Lord" (Isaiah 60:6).

A Bimillennial Tribute

Practically everyone has heard of John 3:16, "For God so loved the world that he gave his Son . . . " But equally true is

John 3:35 which says that God so loved the Son, He is giving Him the world!

The bimillennial will best be celebrated as it dramatizes the reality of how the Father loves the Son, and is now bringing Him the world's tribute, honor and glory.

Webster defines "tribute" in the ancient context of royalty. It is "something given or contributed voluntarily as due or deserved, especially: a gift or service showing respect, gratitude or affection."

Any movement of spiritual procession that arises from our cities unto Christ in light of His bimillennial needs to be seen against this larger canvas of tribute and honor being brought to the Son.[3] The bimillennial is not just the commemoration of a man. It is also the celebration of the lordship of Christ, through the nations going up to the New Jerusalem.

We live in a cynical age which has lost the high concept of what it means to *honor* another or pay homage to one who is worthy. We are so used to public officials or religious leaders serving with *dishonor*, we might sometimes find it foreign to think of honoring anyone. Ours is a culture without genuine heroes. Even Superman has died! But there are signs the tide might turn.

Shine, Jesus, Shine

Since 1987, millions of people around the world have sung the chorus called "Shine, Jesus, Shine" written by one of England's most popular worship leader, Graham Kendrick. What many people don't know is that this chorus has been the flag song for an epoch making movement of spiritual procession, called March for Jesus.

Spontaneously begun in the Soho district of London in 1985, the March for Jesus is becoming the world's biggest street party. The concept is a simple one. On a designated day of the year in cities across the world, people of all ages, races and traditions fill the streets to joyfully proclaim their faith, pray for their cities and sing praise songs. There is no other agenda. It is simply a gift of praise to Jesus.

I first encountered the March for Jesus movement in 1991. Graham Kendrick came over to the States to share the story of the praise march in Europe. He explained how twenty European countries were planning to march for Jesus in 1992, and invited us, as Americans, to join in.

Upon hearing Graham talk about 1992, I felt the march would be redemptive for the quincentennial year. In 1492, one continent had walked over another. Now five hundred years later, those same two continents would walk together, side by side in Christ.

The March for Jesus vision spread like wildfire across America. A pastor in Virginia felt his city should do a praise march even before he heard about the March for Jesus. He reserved a parade permit for May 23rd. When he learned about March for Jesus, he called the national office in Austin, Texas, only to learn the whole world would join him on that date!

On May 23rd, 1992, more than 600,000 people marched for Jesus in 200 cities around the world. In newly-united Berlin, a crowd of 70,000 marched from East to West Germany, passing through Brandenburg Gate, where Hitler once paraded his troops. In Albania, once opposed to religious liberty, the march started with 200 and ended with 2,000, where a statement was read from the president that recognized how people of faith had helped usher in a new era for that country.

I was helping to organize a "March for Jesus" in Pasadena, Calif. that year. Just three weeks before the praise march, the Los Angeles riots broke out. I went on a "Street Beat" radio program to say, "We've seen what hell can do, now let's give heaven a chance!" Within days, 20,000 marchers in the Los Angeles area filled many of those same streets.

March Gains Momentum

The following year, on June 12, 1993, more than 850 cities worldwide held a "March for Jesus," sweeping more than two

million people into praise marches. The lead song of praise
march expressed our prayer:

> We'll walk the land, with hearts on fire,
> And every step will be a prayer.
> Hope is rising, new day dawning,
> Sound of singing fills the air.
> Two thousand years and still the flame
> Is burning bright across the land.
> Hearts are waiting, longing, aching,
> For awakening once again.[4]
>
> Let the Flame Burn Brighter by Graham Kendrick,
> © 1992 by Make Way Music. Used by Permission.

In our city, one marcher said of the fellowship, "This is
what it's going to be like in heaven." The *Denver Post* hailed
the March for Jesus as "a beginning of festivities leading to the
commemoration of the 2,000th anniversary of Christ's birth."

The March for Jesus movement is not a protest, nor a
political event, but a praise march. We march for our cities and
for our future as given by God.

Marches today have become everyday news. Everybody
seems to be marching these days, against something or against
somebody. It seems any group with an agenda is marching to
show their strength and to appeal for acceptance.

Parades used to celebrate our shared culture, now marches
have become vehicles to legitimize our status as victims.
Marches spill into our streets, and escalate the fight for
attention, sympathy, money and legal protection.

Contrast this with the March for Jesus. It is not a media
event. It has no social or political agenda. It is not marching
against anything, but rather to someone. As Tom Pelton, U.S.
march organizer states, "There may be spectators, there may
not. We march for an audience of one."

A worship march like this leaves healing behind where
there was once hurt, faith where fear once ruled and hope where
despair once reigned. I see the March for Jesus movement as

a sign that says this is not the end of the road. There is hope, if we walk together. As the third millennium dawns, this "train is bound for glory!"

The March for Jesus movement convened its largest praise march yet on June 25, 1994. On that day a march circled the globe with more than ten million people in the streets with public praise. It started in Seoul, Korea with one million people, then swept from time zone to time zone, in one city after another worldwide. In one Pacific time zone, where there are no islands, a praise march was held by sailors on the deck of a U.S. Naval vessel!

I see this as nothing less than an epoch-making march in response to the call of the Spirit of God. More than anything else, these historic processions may keep our focus on Christ as we approach the bimillennial.

Tell Your Grandchildren

Graham Kendrick has written the early story of the March for Jesus movement in the book *Public Praise*.[5]

Wisely, the March for Jesus movement is re-envisioned each time it is done. If the movement lasts until the year 2000, and all signs point to that possibility, it could be one of the few holidays solely for Jesus that we have not totally commercialized.

I have a hunch that our heavenly Father is so eager to honor Jesus in the bimillennial, He has allowed the March for Jesus movement to be born early in cities around the world to insure that one great offering of praise is gathered from the East to the West to present to our Lord on His 2,000th birthday.

I believe in 20 years, we will look back and tell our grandchildren about the March for Jesus movement saying, "Yes, I was there when the bimillennial era began. We marched for Jesus all the way up Congress Avenue. From 1996 to 2001, it became the 'March of the Millennium'—the march that led up to the bimillennial, the Jubilee year of 2000—when the church celebrated the 2,000th anniversary of the birth of the world's only Savior."

And when they had opened their treasures,
they presented unto him gifts;
gold, and frankincense, and myrrh.
—Matthew 2:11

10

The Celebration
of Civilization

While shifting through the treasures of civilization, historian Arnold Toynbee once wrote "the works of artists and men of letters outlive the deeds of businessmen, soldiers and statesmen. The poets and the philosophers outrange the historians; while the prophets and the saints overtop and outlast them all."[1] Surely the person of Jesus, as a prophet and a saint, is the greatest treasure of all.

People through the ages have recognized this and created their own memorials to celebrate the life of Jesus. Whether icons or frescoes, monasteries or cathedrals, each generation has treasured Christ in its own unique way.

The bimillennial is now upon us—the most significant celebration in the history of civilization. What can our generation do to celebrate the memory and life of this man which has so marked world history?

The Banquet of Life

Several years ago, I had the opportunity to meet Graham Kerr, the Galloping Gourmet. He is the consummate host, serving up a spectacular meal with kindness and humor. Recently, I spoke with him by phone about how whole cities might celebrate 2000. Graham said something that stuck with me: "Wouldn't it be marvelous if every city in America would celebrate the year 2000 together with a sister city from the Third World?"

This desire to invite the poor to join our occasions of celebration was also Jesus' passion. When honored over dinner, Jesus said to his Pharisee host, "But when you give a banquet, invite the poor, the crippled, the lame, the blind, and you will be blessed" (Luke 14:13).

He then told the story of how a landowner prepared a great banquet, only to have his friends refuse his invitation. The owner got so furious, he sent his servants into the alleys of the town and the countryside lanes to bring in the poor.

As we prepare to honor Jesus during His bimillennial, we need to insure that the millions across our world which have been denied access to our human occasions of celebration receive a genuine invitation to what I call the "Celebration of Civilization," or Christ's banquet of life.

The Unfinished Task

Tradition tells us the twelve apostles took the gospel of Jesus to the known world of their day. Through the centuries the church has continued this apostolic work of establishing communities of faith among the nations. Today, people gather to worship Jesus Christ as Lord in every country. One third of our world's population considers themselves Christian. Millions more live in societies which have churches.

Yet for every three people on this planet who have access to the gospel, there is one person who has little to no opportunity to know Christ. They usually lack a Bible in their language, Christian radio broadcasts, or nearby local church.

In 1989, I visited Dr. David Barrett, mission statistician and "computer prophet" of world evangelization. He had just published his projections for Christian missions for the period of 1990 to 2000. Across the hall from his office, Dr. Barrett had a huge wall-sized world map on which he had drawn a great "unevangelized belt."

A thick black boundary line cut across Soviet Central Asia, curved downward to include the western minorities of China, jutted out to encompass Indonesia, then swung back to include North India, North Africa, only to end finally in the Middle East. For years Christian leaders had talked about unreached peoples, now Barrett was mapping their domain.

Over lunch, Barrett explained, "In this belt there are more than 170 groups of a million or more people that are unevangelized." As a bloc, Barrett said they represent 24 percent of the world's population. Each year this group receives less than 5 percent of the world's income.

For many, inadequate shelter, malnutrition, illiteracy, disease and unemployment are ways of life. Many of the unreached are also materially impoverished.

The Cradle of Civilization

Since Barrett first introduced his research, others have designated this belt as the "10/40 window," a massive corridor of need which lies north of the equator, between the tenth and fortieth parallels, cutting across Africa, the Middle East and Asia.

The amazing thing about this 10/40 window is that it encompasses the original cradlelands of civilization, where the oldest emerged some 6,000 years ago, whether Sumer, Egypt, India or China.

Recently I attended a public lecture on NAFTA, the North American Free Trade Agreement. The lecturer had done work for the World Bank in Kenya and Pakistan. Afterwards, I asked him, "We have been talking about economic communities and trading zones in Western Europe, East Asia and North America. What about Africa, the Middle East and Central Asia?" He regretfully responded, "It may take forty years to see these regions stabilize and grow to the point that they can compete in our world economy."

It's tragic that the cradle of civilization is still in diapers when it comes to joining the world economy.

As the Cold War has faded, it is clear that we face not a "new world order" but a fractured and troubled planet. The East-West clash of ideology may be fading, but the North-South economic gap is widening.

As Yale economist Paul Kennedy writes, there are firms and nations, largely in the Northern hemisphere, that are well positioned for economic growth in the years ahead. Their prospects are the basis for many optimistic works that forecast humanity's ever-increasing prosperity.

On the other hand, Kennedy notes the many pessimist writings that deal with population explosion and environmental catastrophes among developing countries. He writes there are "billions of impoverished, uneducated individuals in the developing world . . . whose prospects are poor, and in many cases, getting worse."

Initially, it might seem only one school of thought is right, but it could be, as Kennedy says, they are both correct, only describing different aspects of a single phenomena so that "the optimists are excited about the world's 'winners' whereas the pessimists worry at the fate of the 'losers.'"

Kennedy sees the gap steadily widening between the rich and poor as we enter the next century, leading not only to social unrest within developing countries, but global political tensions, mass migration and environmental damage from which "even the 'winners' might not emerge unscathed."[2]

In Jesus' eyes, whether spiritually or economically, the poor are the lost coins, the lost sheep, the prodigal sons of our day and age. Those with an open heart will search them out and invite them back to the Father's table. Indeed, the cradle of civilization needs a fresh invitation to Christ's celebration of civilization as we prepare for the bimillennial.

Pray for the Gift-Bearers

In October 1993, more than 20 million people around the world participated in "praying through the window." For some it meant a prayer journey among the 10/40 window, for most it meant a month of concerted prayer that God might bring forth new treasures from the unreached world.

If our prayers would be answered as we look to the year 2000, what might come forth from the cradle of civilization? Surely we would pray for enduring peace between Palestinians and Jews. We might hope for self-government for the Kurdish people, who suffered so much at the hand of Sadam Hussein after the Gulf War.

My highest prayer is for another journey of the wise men to arise, a spiritual procession of gift-bearers coming forth from the cradle of civilization to follow the Star of 2000.

The story of the Magi has become so much a part of our Christmas tradition, we sometimes forget that the original Magi were not Jewish, but seekers from the Gentile world. Alerted by a cosmic occurrence, they embarked on a spiritual pilgrimage to pay tribute to the newborn King. Scriptures say when they saw the Child, "they bowed down and worshiped him. Then they opened treasures and presented him with gifts of gold and of incense and of myrrh" (Matthew 2:11).

In seeing the Child, they recognized something in Him which transcended their own culture and tradition, worthy of the best treasures their world had to offer.

Unbegun Relationships

In speaking about the year 2000, I prefer to talk more about starting "unbegun relationships" than completing the "unfinished task." When I hear about Muslims in Turkey, or Hindus in India, it seems my world and theirs are so far apart. I wonder, what do we have in common? How would I talk about Jesus if we ever met? If I did, would they possibly hear and understand my witness?

While these are valid questions, I've begun to ask a more profound one in relationship to Jesus' bimillennial. I ask, "What potential gift do these people have which will one day be brought to God through Christ?"

We need to move beyond thinking about people in terms of ministry "targets" or "windows."

These are individuals of great value who have been denied access to our human occasions of celebration. They must, in our time, receive a genuine invitation to Jesus' banquet of life, not just for what they can receive, but also for what they can give.

As we look to the bimillennial, we need to catch a vision of the tremendous glory, beauty and dignity the people of the world have and can bring before God in honor of Christ.

Quit the Race, Find the Grace

This contrast between finishing the "unfinished task" versus starting "unbegun relationships" came into focus for me about two years ago when a former student of ours, Sandi Turner, took Olgy and me out to dinner at the Peppermill restaurant.

After we met Sandi at UCLA in 1985, she headed off for China as a teacher, only to come home after four years.

Over gourmet soups and marinated steaks, we spent a wonderful evening together reminiscing about old times. Then the conversation turned to what life was like for her after China. "It hasn't been easy being back. I came home from China drained. I've been in counseling for two years. Only in the last six months have I started to find myself."

Sandi went on to share how she came from a dysfunctional home. At age five she turned off her emotions. That was a coping mechanism to survive.

With her emotions turned off she resigned to go the long haul. She developed a habit to finish everything she started. That was her way of getting satisfaction.

This compulsion for completion was what attracted her to go to China and help complete the "unfinished task."

"When I left my work in China unfinished, I felt like a failure," Sandi shared, "but recently I have begun to rethink things."

"After training hard for a marathon last month, I decided not to compete three days before it started due to tendinitis. You know what? For the first time in my life it was OK not to finish something. Before I discovered my emotions, I would have stuck it out, despite the pain."

Sandi taught me a lesson that night. It is OK to drop out of the race if it leads you to celebrate God's grace. She began to pursue afresh the "unbegun relationships" in her life, with herself, her vocation, the Lord and the larger international community.

A year later, I heard Sandi was planning to return to China. This time she was, no doubt, better able to invite others to Jesus' celebration of civilization.

An All-Nations Celebration

Jesus was always ready to initiate these "unbegun relationships" with those from the international community. Although His mission was directed to the Jews, He went out of His way to celebrate life with people who normally were excluded from Jewish social occasions. I love the story of Jesus' encounter with the Roman centurion in Capernaum for this reason.

The Gospel of Luke tells us that a household servant of this Roman officer was about to die. Instead of coming directly to Jesus, the centurion appealed to Jesus through leaders of the Jewish community.

When Jesus heard of the servant boy's need, He immediately dropped what He was doing and began to walk toward the centurions' house.

Jesus was not far from the house, when the centurion sent friends to say, "Lord, don't trouble yourself, for I do not deserve to have you come under my roof. That is why I did not even consider myself worthy to come to you. But say the word, and my servant will be healed." The centurion knew the power of a military commander, so he reasoned that Jesus, likewise, had charge over angels to carry out his commands. He only asked for Jesus to give the healing word.

Astonished by this Gentile's extraordinary faith, Jesus turned to the crowd following Him and said, "I tell you the truth, I have not found anyone in Israel with such great faith."

In a moment, Jesus gave the word to heal his servant boy, but not before sharing with the Jews gathered around him, "I say to you that many will come from the east and the west, and will take their places at the feast with Abraham, Isaac and Jacob in the kingdom of heaven" (Matthew 8:10, 11).

At the end of history, believers from all generations will gather from all nations to eat and dine at the feast of Jesus. The Roman centurion is sure to be there as well, eager to share his tribute to Jesus.

The Riches of Culture

Oftentimes we have to rediscover the gospel in order to help another culture unlock the gifts they have for God. This was certainly true in the case of Vincent Donovan, a Roman Catholic priest who worked among the Masai people of West Africa. He shares about his journey in the book *Christianity Rediscovered*.

After a year of work in Tanzania, Donovan found the influence of the Catholic Mission very strong in the Loliondo region, but their relationship with the Masai people had to do with schools, hospitals or cattle, not with Christ.

Donovan asked permission from his Bishop to leave the institutions and just go and talk to the pagan Masai about God and see what, if anything, would happen.

He first approached an influential Masai elder, named Ndangoya. He reminded the elder that the Padres were well known for their work in schools and hospitals, but he no longer

wanted to talk about these. He had come to talk about God in
the life of the Masai. Indeed, that was why he had come from
America. Ndangoya, the Masai elder, looked puzzled for a long
time and then said, "If that is why you came here, why did you
wait so long to tell us about this?"

Thus began a weekly dialogue between Ndangoya's people
and Donovan. Over the next year, Donovan shared many stories with the Masai, all of which pointed to Jesus as the lion
of the clan of Judah.

The time came when Donovan came to the end of the good
news. It was now their decision. They could accept or reject
Jesus.

Donovan came back the next week. The old man,
Ndangoya, stood up and said, "From the first day I have spoken
for these people . . . Now, on this day one year later, I can declare
for them and for all this community, that we have reached the
step in our lives where we can say, 'We believe.'"

We believe. Communal faith. Donovan, who was raised in
a western, American culture, was so geared to individual
decisions he had never thought that a whole community could
embrace Christ through faith. But they did.

Rather than leave their vast, all-pervasive complex of customs, traditions and values, they brought these to Christ. The
Eucharist in the Masai communities took an open and free
form. In many cases it was joyous, festive and embraced all of
the neighborhood in which it was celebrated.

Instead of limited to a church building, the celebration
usually started in the place where the elders lighted their fires
and proceeded to the area where dancing was always held in
the village.

Within a short period of time, the good news of Jesus was
embraced by more than 3,000 believers among many Masai
communities. To give direction to these communities,
Donovan reports that a general council of the Masai elders of
the Brotherhood of Christ emerged.

One of the elders, named Keriko, stood up and said: "We should be grateful that the Word of Jesus has come to us at a time when so many things in Masai life are going bad . . . The Word of God has come to save the beautiful things we have in our customs, and do away with the evil that has grown among us. As I see the Word of Jesus and the Brotherhood—they are come to make us better Masai."[3]

The Masai's story teach us that the cultures of the world with all their riches and treasures are not destined merely for salvation or conservation, but transformation. They are to be lifted up, fulfilled and transformed in the celebration of Christ.

The Wedding Supper

One of the most meaningful days of my life was my wedding day in 1978. Following the service and receiving line at church, we went to our wedding reception.

As I looked out from the head table, I remember thinking, "If this is so wonderful, just think of what the wedding supper of heaven will be like." I could see all of our family and friends, those I grew up with, and those I met later in life.

Each year Olgy and I watch a video of our wedding, and each guest we see triggers a different memory of the goodness of God in our lives.

Scriptures speak of the coming kingdom banquet as the wedding supper of the Lamb. It will be a celebration of the grace of God in civilization, throughout history.

Imagine the stories that will be told by Abraham, Moses and Elijah, or Isaiah, Ruth, Daniel or King Nebuchadnezzar. Imagine the stories you will tell. Like the proverbial Knights of the Round Table, we will take our place at the banquet. Jesus will be our guest of honor, and the toast of all nations.

No wonder the angel said to John the apostle, "Blessed are those who are invited to the wedding supper of the Lamb!" (Revelation 19:9). The coming bimillennial should be no less than an international celebration of civilization in honor of Jesus.

Do This in Remembrance of Me

Lately, as I have meditated on the meaning of the wedding supper of the Lamb, I put aside the high tech vision of vast crowds at city convention centers celebrating the bimillennial through satellite hookups. The question came to me: "Did Jesus ever ask us to remember Him? If so, in what way?"

I immediately thought of Jesus, how on the night before the cross, He took the cup, gave thanks and shared it with His friends. Then He took the bread, gave thanks and divided it among His disciples. He said, "This is my body given for you; do this in remembrance of me."

Through this simple act, Jesus asked us to remember Him, to celebrate Him if you will.

Whoever partakes of the Lord's Supper participates in a commemorative Eucharist celebration. They look to the past in grateful, believing memory for the broken body and shed blood of Jesus. They affirm the New Covenant in the present through a community meal with Jesus in their midst. They point to the meal at the consummation of the kingdom in the future, when all nations will join the wedding supper of the Lamb.

Celebrating the Lord's Supper then is perhaps the most prophetic thing we can do to commemorate Christ in light of His bimillennial. It is the heart and soul of the celebration of civilization.

Knowing our sophisticated media culture, it is all but certain the bimillennial will energize consumerism around the world. Hopefully, our sacred celebrations will not put the accent on consumption or technology, but look toward the consummation in Christ.

And, if we practice the "banquet etiquette" toward the poor as Jesus prescribed, our pilgrimages, pageants, or prayer vigils will honor Him with all the glory that our culture can bring, in the midst of the communion celebration Jesus instituted.

Better to light one candle
than to curse the darkness.
—Chinese proverb

11

Light Two
Thousand Candles

Andy Lakey could have easily died through a drug overdose on New Year's Day in 1986. Instead, he gained a new life, new faith, even a new career. "As my spirit hovered between heaven and earth, angels started to swirl around my feet and one wrapped his arms around me."

Andy doesn't know whether he heard words or not, but through this heavenly messenger, he felt the reassurance, peace and care of a loving God. "The immense strength of that angel flowed through me, healing me, restoring me to life," Andy shares, "and then the experience softly dissolved, and my spirit was reunited with my body."

"My real life didn't begin until that day." Andy remembers waking up, with his vision and insight sharper than it had ever been. He looked back on the first twenty-seven years of life, and saw how much he had wasted.

Rather than be devastated by this realization, he felt empowered to leave his old life due to the sign of God's love he received. "I knew that with the support of my friends, I could—and would—try to give something back to God in thanks for my life having been given back to me. And I had a sense that my future was going to be wonderful, although I wasn't sure in which way."

During recovery, Andy's faith began to deepen. He began to draw and paint, especially angels. He never studied art formally, but his mother and grandfather were artists, so he grew up with an understanding of art.

When he turned 30, it was as if his angel tapped him on the shoulder and said, "You're doing fine, Andy, now please make a sharp right turn here on the highway of life." He left his well-paying job and turned his garage into an art studio. His boss told him he was crazy, but something inside gave him strength.

"I could still see in my mind's eye the angel that had wrapped his arms around me to comfort and reassure me three years before. I wanted, I needed to share that sense of peace and strength with others."

The Angel 2000 Series

Andy decided to give witness to God who sends angels into our lives. "I decided to paint two thousand angels by the year 2000—one angel for each year since Jesus was born." Whereas before, it used to take him hours to make a preliminary sketch, he found inspiration coming instantly for his angel themes. "It's as though I am tapping into the universe, tapping into God. My talent is 'on loan' from God."

Andy's first angel painting now hangs in the Vatican. The third belongs to former President Jimmy Carter. Dozens of others grace the homes of Hollywood or sport stars such as Gloria Estefan, Dudley Moore, Quincey Jones, Arnold Palmer, Mickey Mantle, Stevie Wonder and Ray Charles. Andy says his paintings even hang in hospitals and clinics, and centers for the blind.

Yes, blind people! Many of the Angel 2000 paintings are three-dimensional. Andy lays the paint on in such a thick way that anyone can feel the painting and trace the outlines, sensing through touch the love that once touched Andy.

In fact, many of the Angel 2000 series are purchased to donate to others who are sight-impaired. Peter Jennings has donated one to The Lighthouse in New York city, Lee Meriwether has given one to the Blind Children's Center, and former President Gerald Ford and his wife, Betty, have donated one Angel painting to the Betty Ford Clinic.

"I feel that something incredible should happen in the year 2000. That's why I have set out to create 2,000 individual paintings." Andy intends to complete his series in time for the bimillennial.

In view of the greatest Christmas ever, Andy has launched an "Angel Project" to benefit children. If you do a "random act of kindness" for any child, anywhere, the Angel Gallery in Portland, Ore. will send you, free, a miniature angel painting to hang or wear as a pin. Once you receive your pin, the Angel Gallery offers you a free Andy Lakey angel painting, worth $500, if you give $100 or 10 hours of work to your favorite children's charity.

Andy's good deeds campaign is a fitting tribute to those angelic messengers who announced the Advent in Bethlehem by singing, "Glory to God in the highest, and on earth peace, good will toward men."

It's Jesus' Birthday!

I often tell others that the bimillennial will be the world's biggest birthday party in honor of the world's greatest leader. When my daughter, Christine, was in pre-school, she brought this point home to me. One day, right before Christmas, Christine's teacher asked the class, "What is Christmas all about?" After a few replies, Christine felt the obvious had been overlooked. She shot up her little 4-year-old hand, and upon being recognized said, "Don't you know? Christmas is Jesus' birthday!"

Birthdays are one of our most beautiful traditions. From the time each of us is in diapers, we celebrate our birthday. As time passes we attend the birthday parties of our friends. As always, our mom tucks a little gift under our arms to give to the special birthday boy or girl.

As each year goes by, I aim to be simpler. I find myself now looking at 2000 with child-like eyes and asking, "What gift could I give the Lord Jesus on this special occasion of His 2,000th birthday?"

Light the Night

In preparation for Jesus' 2,000th birthday, we should aim to light a candle, rather than curse the darkness. Chuck Colson grew up thinking that powerful people shaped history. He determined to leave his mark on history by influencing the most powerful institution he could think of: the presidency of the United States.

Yet, four years after he reached the office next to the President, he was frustrated and disillusioned. As Watergate unfolded, everything he sought to build was crumbling. The most powerful people in America became bogged down in a bungled burglary.

Colson went to prison for this, but through a renewal of faith in Christ, he was set free in his spirit. He came to a new way of thinking, namely, that history is most often influenced not by grand pronouncements and programs of political leaders, but by ordinary people.

Before the phrase "a thousand points of light" was made popular, Colson saw that the "world's darkness is illuminated not by grand spotlights, but by a thousand points of light flickering in the night"—individual people living out God's love among those in need.[1]

As we look to the year 2000, we must learn the wisdom of the ancient Chinese proverb: "It is better to light one candle than to curse the darkness." Each of us, wherever we are, can light a candle in honor of Jesus' 2,000th birthday to illuminate the darkness. Two thousand candles will not be sufficient to celebrate the bimillennial. We need millions of little lights to honor the Light of the World.

Twenty-Five Ways to Light a Candle

You don't need to have a brush with death to be inspired to bring a gift to the Star of 2000. Here are 25 little ways to light a candle for Christ by the year 2000. Many of these ideas relate to keeping a candle lit in your *heart*. That is where it must start. We must light a fire for Jesus in our soul, and fan the flame until we are whole. From there, it can warm our home, church or community.

1. Meditate on the names of Jesus.

Our spiritual procession to the year 2000 should begin with a rebirth of praise in our hearts for the Lord Jesus. In this area, I have found the names of Jesus to be helpful. The Scriptures call him Wonderful Counselor, Mighty God, Everlasting Father and Prince of Peace.

About two years ago, my wife gave me a devotional called *The Wonderful Names of Our Wonderful Lord*.[2] It contains 365 verses, from Genesis to Revelation, each with a brief comment. Reflecting on some attribute of Jesus is a great way to start your day and discover the "unsearchable riches of Christ" as we approach the bimillennial.

2. Display a book about Jesus on your coffee table.

Another way to remind yourself and family of the coming bimillennial is to display a book on Jesus in your living room. One of the most treasured Christmas gifts I ever received was from my sister Suzanne. It was a unique pictorial narrative of the life of Jesus, entitled *His Face*.[3] Although nowhere in the gospels is the physical appearance of Jesus described, the world's artists have sought for twenty centuries to portray

Christ's essential qualities of divinity and humanity. *His Face* captures 95 unique portraits of Christ. Another bimillennial picture book is *Jesus 2000* by Lion Publishing.[4] Soon every major publisher will likely release a commemorative book on Jesus as we approach the 2,000th anniversary of His birth.

3. Build a file of quotes or poems about Jesus.

Through the centuries, the pen, not just the paintbrush, has been used to honor Christ. I have a folder in my desk, along with a file in my computer, where I keep tributes to Jesus, whether quotes, or poems.

My heart has always been filled with wonder as I read the poem, "One Solitary Life." Without using Jesus' name, it recounts His obscure background and sacrificial death. It concludes, "All the armies that ever marched, all the navies that ever sailed, all the parliaments that ever sat, all the kings that every reigned, put together, have not affected the life of man on this earth as much as that One Solitary Life."

What are your favorite tributes to Christ? Collect them, hang them on your walls and share them with others. My wife loves the popular "I AM" poster, listing the names of Jesus. She has three hanging in our house.

I post things in and around my computer. With the help of a computer Bible program, my file is filled with what the writers of the New Testament had to say about Jesus, quotes on Jesus from great leaders in history, as well as prose by other writers.

4. Memorize portions of Jesus' words.

You could go a step further and memorize a portion of Jesus' words from the New Testament. Many scholars tell us Jesus probably had His disciples commit much of His teachings to memory, in the tradition of rabbinical teaching. What better way to commemorate the bimillennial than to memorize some portion of Jesus' words. Then look for opportunities to share your rendition.

A close friend of mine recently heard a speaker share from memory Jesus' "Sermon on the Mount." It left a deep impression on her. A variation of this idea is to create or buy simple pamphlets which share Jesus' promises and commemorate His bimillennial.

5. Play praise tapes which exalt Christ.

Another way we keep a candle lit for Christ in our hearts is by playing praise tapes at home or in the car. In the past 15 years so many of the new choruses or hymns address the Lord in worship, rather than each other. I am thinking of "Majesty" by Jack Hayford, or "El Shaddai," as sung by Amy Grant.

Putting on a praise tape helps me restore my focus, and allows me to enter into spiritual procession and celebrate Jesus. A good source for praise tapes is *Hosanna Integrity Music.* Check your local Christian bookstore.

6. Celebrate the liturgical seasons in your home.

Each day, week and year needs to be a boot camp of celebration in view of the coming bimillennial. As we learn how to celebrate the smaller units of life—this will bring meaning to the larger global occasions, especially the greatest Christmas ever.

The liturgical church calendar allows you to celebrate the life of Christ in a visual and audio way, starting from His birth, through His ministry on earth, His death, resurrection and the coming of the Holy Spirit.

The Christian calendar grew out of our Jewish heritage. It was only natural for Christians to observe their Sabbath on the first day of week, Sunday, and celebrate Jesus' resurrection.

In time, they substituted Easter for Passover, and substituted Pentecost—the coming of the Holy Spirit—for the giving of the Law of Moses on Mt. Sinai. With the addition of the Advent season, the church year, as we know it, was fully developed by the sixth century.

Three resources can help in this area. The first is *The*

Irrational Season by popular author, Madeleine L'Engle.[5] In her warm, story-telling fashion, she shares her experience of celebrating the liturgical season. A more practical book on the church year and a great guide for families is *Dull Dinners into Sacred Feasts.*[6] This little manual gives wonderful guidelines, recipes, and home service suggestions for celebrating the various holidays. A third resource of this kind is entitled *Making Sunday Special* by Karen Mains.[7] If you are looking for renewed meaning to your work and leisure, Mains' book helps you restore a sense of wonder and awe to your week by helping your family celebrate each Sunday in a special way. This is especially needed as we approach the Jubilee year of 2000.

7. Throw a birthday party for Jesus.

Several years ago, Gail Reese of Cleveland, Ohio, noticed that Christmas Day would fall on Sunday. In response, she planned a big birthday party for Jesus complete with balloons and cake. The highlight of the day came when children sang "Happy Birthday" to Jesus, and then offered thanks for the gift of God's Son.

You don't have to wait until Christmas falls on Sunday to do this. This idea can work very well in your home the second or third week of December. As a group, you might exchange gifts, or make greeting cards which express your devotion to Christ. Be creative.

8. Hold a Jesus block party in your neighborhood.

Another way to celebrate the life of Jesus is through the *JESUS* film. More than 600 million people have seen this unique film on Jesus, based entirely on the book of Luke. Now New Life Resources has released a special 77-minute version of the *JESUS* film on video-cassette.

It makes for a perfect culmination of a neighborhood block party, especially before the Christmas or Easter holidays. It can also be done at other times. Recently, forty churches in my city joined hands to distribute the *JESUS* video to every unchurched home in our area. A complete *JESUS* home video kit, with hints on how to do the same, is available by calling 1-800-827-2788.

9. Have a Jesus film festival in your home.

The most meaningful Easter holiday we ever had as a family was watching Franco Zeffirelli's *Jesus of Nazareth* on video. After an early sunrise service, we put out a spread of dips and sandwiches on our dining room table and viewed this stunning six-hour movie.

Our good family friend, Barbara, who spent the day with us, found our family "film festival" to be her most meaningful Easter ever. Since then we have continued this Jesus film festival as a family tradition. Check your local video store for this three-tape series.

10. Attend a regional worship symposium.

A worship symposium is a one- to two-day conference just for the purpose of worship! It's not just for musicians, but for anyone who desires to be a worshiper in spirit and truth.

Besides large group worship sessions, there usually are workshops covering a whole range of topics from "Praise in the Psalms," to "Pageantry and Banner Procession," or "Tambourine" or "Drama" clinics for kids and teenagers.

Some ministries which conduct national or regional praise and worship conferences include: the International Worship Symposium, the annual Christian Artist Seminar, Kent Henry Ministries, Lamar Boschman's International Worship Leaders' Institute, or North American Liturgical Resources.

11. Join a march for Jesus.

Another way to join the spiritual procession gaining momentum in light of Jesus' bimillennial is through participating in a city-wide praise march. On June 25th, 1994, more than 1,000 cities hosted a "March for Jesus" sweeping more than ten million people worldwide into one grand living, moving praise march unto Christ.

In a "March for Jesus" people of all ages and traditions come together one day of the year to openly declare their love for the Lord through praise, prayer and proclamations. Usually they walk and sing along a 10-block route to the heart of their city.

Originally conceived in London, the March for Jesus movement has spread to more than 100 countries. It is really a moving festival of praise and worship in the streets, and could become by the year 2000, the last holiday solely for Jesus that we haven't entirely commercialized! To find a "March for Jesus" in your area, contact: March for Jesus U.S.A., P.O. Box 3216, Austin, TX 78764-3216, (512) 416-0066.

12. Participate in a concert of prayer.

We experience prayer on many meaningful levels, through personal devotions, before meals, in corporate worship, or small group Bible studies. As we approach the bimillennial, people will likely gather for united city-wide prayer in unique prayer events called Concerts of Prayer.

In Concerts of Prayer people from various denominations and traditions gather to pray for the *fullness* of Christ as Lord in the church, and the *fulfillment* of Christ's purposes through the church among the nations.

For resources or information on a prayer concert in your area contact: Concerts of Prayer International, P.O. Box 1399, Wheaton, IL 60189-1399, (708) 690-8441.

For information on the National Day of Prayer in the United States, each year on the first Thursday in May, contact: National Day of Prayer, P.O. Box 15616, Colorado Springs, CO 80935-5616, (719) 531-3379.

13. Attend or present a play which dramatizes Jesus.

For the past 20 years, Jesus has become a pop star through productions like "Jesus Christ Superstar" or "Godspell." Now as the bimillennial nears, more and more performing arts groups will take to the road in "Jesus" productions.

Recently, "Jesus Was His Name," a traveling entertainment extravaganza, combining 58 live actors with filmed scenes on an 80-foot screen, toured 32 major cities of America. Created by French director Robert Hossein, "Jesus" premiered in Paris, where it played to 600,000 people over the period of 18 months. "I wanted to proclaim my faith in this world and my faith in man," said Hossein in a press release. "I wanted to do so through the words of Christ, for He remains the conscience of humanity."

In most areas, either during the holidays, or throughout summer, various production companies perform passion plays or dramas about the life of Christ. Getting youth involved in a Christmas or Easter play can also awaken them to Jesus and His bimillennial. Your local production might not be sponsored by New York's Radio City Music Hall, but it can bring Jesus to life for those in your community.

"The Promise" (by Jan Dargatz and Gary Rhodes), distributed by Word Music, is a popular production on Jesus for local drama groups.

14. Reenact the journey of the Magi.

Another relevant way to point to the Star of 2000, particularly during the Advent season, is by coordinating a bimillennial reenactment of the journey of the Magi. Ever since the days of St. Francis, people have been filled with awe and wonder by gazing on Christ through a living nativity scene.

In coordination with the Journey of the Magi 2000 commemoration project in the Middle East, hundreds of cities around the world from 1998 to 2001 will reenact their own journey of the Magi in their area through spiritual processions, nativity scenes, Wise Men plays, and Epiphany services.

If you are interested in sponsoring a commemoration in your area contact: Journey of the Magi 2000, P.O. Box 1037, Pinecrest, CA 95634, (209) 586-2000.

15. Discover Jesus' place in history and culture.

In preparation for the celebration of centuries, you might discover how Jesus has impacted each age and epoch over the past twenty centuries. The most original study in this area is *Jesus Through the Centuries* by Jaroslav Pelikan. It can be found in most libraries. This book looks at history's most intriguing figure and His enormous impact on cultural, political, social and economic history. It makes for compelling reading for anyone on the eve of the 2,000th anniversary of the birth of Jesus.

Another must-read book is *Jesus: The Man Who Lives* by Malcolm Muggeridge, the distinguished international British journalist. Muggeridge opens his book with this simple, yet profound, line: "The coming of Jesus into the world is the most stupendous event in human history."

16. Discover the cultural history of the bimillennium.

In addition to commemorating Jesus' history during the bimillennial, society will celebrate the cultural history of the past twenty centuries.

From the dawn of civilization, people have asked the great questions, such as, "How can God be known?," "What is good, beautiful, and true?" or "How can liberty, equality, and justice be guarded by society?"

Lately, I have been reading the great books of world civilization with this question in mind: "In what ways has the great conversation of civilization been a reflection of the great ideals of Jesus?"

One helpful guide to this general cultural history can usually be found at a public library. *The Great Ideas* is a two-volume set which gives an overview of the 102 great ideas of Western civilization and how the "great books" address these issues.[8]

Many public libraries also offer a "great books reading and discussion program" which you can join.

17. Write a paper on the bimillennial.

Are you currently taking a class, or teaching one? Consider writing a paper on the bimillennial celebrations of the year 2000. It can be looked at from many vantage points. In the Social Sciences you might write about "The Role of Celebration in Society." In history, you might investigate "The Age of Anniversaries: bicentennial to bimillennial." If you are studying religion, a paper on "Roman Catholic Holy Years and 2000" could be fascinating. If theology is your focus, you could research "Public Praise and 2000."

If you are a budding writer, focus an article on Jesus, or His celebrations in the year 2000. Hundreds of articles and dozens of new books came out on Columbus as we approached his quincentennial. The same will happen with reference to the bimillennial and Jesus. If you get something published, or get a good grade on a paper, please send me a copy!

18. Use your computer to talk 2000.

Are you one of the 20 million people connected to an online computer service like CompuServe, DELPHI, GEnie, Internet, MCI Mail or Prodigy? Consider using an appropriate forum, roundtable or newsgroup to exchange views and information on the bimillennial.

In a trivia oriented forum, just the question of "When does the new millennium begin— January 1, 2000 or 2001?" could generate a landslide of electronic discussions. A scholarly forum might address the social implications of a mega-anniversary, or Jesus' impact on 2,000 years of cultural history. A city-wide computer bulletin board might be a great place to carry on a discussion about how your area might celebrate the "greatest Christmas ever."

I can send you a list of bimillennial topics to help jump start your online discussions. Drop me a message at my Internet address: begin@rainbow.sosi.com and I'll send a list back to you via electronic mail.

19. Visit the Holy Land.

As we approach the 2,000th anniversary of Jesus' birth, millions will want to walk where Jesus walked and visit the Holy Land. A two-week bimillennial tour of Israel could change your life. Imagine tracing the footsteps of Jesus firsthand, from Bethlehem to Nazareth, from Capernaum to Jericho, from Jerusalem and Calvary to the Sea of Galilee.

Not only would you return with a greater understanding of the Bible, but you would grow in your appreciation for how Jesus touched people along the paths of everyday life. I have several friends who, after their first trip to the Holy Land, make return visits with their family or friends.

A good resource in this area is Jesus 2000, launched in January 1994 to host commemorative congresses and tours for Christians to Israel. For information, contact Jesus 2000, P.O. Box 2510, Chattanooga, TN 37409-2510, (615) 821-3635.

20. Be a "celebrate 2000" advocate with the media.

Gone is the day when television, radio or newspapers just reported on current events. Today's media now plays a central role in selecting, shaping and prioritizing the public discussion. As we approach the bimillennial, hundreds of grassroots citizens will be needed to encourage the media to turn their spotlight on Jesus.

It could start with a call to your favorite radio talk show, a letter to the editor at the local newspaper, or lunch with an elected official. Another step could be gifting your public library with a copy of this book, or placing this book in the hands of your local religion page editor. As interest develops, you might form a "celebrate 2000" speakers bureau for your city, or organize a news conference on Jesus' bimillennial.

21. Give a talk on the year 2000.

Do you belong to a professional club or civic group, like the Kiwanas or Rotary Club? Consider making a presentation on the year 2000 and the celebrations of Jesus' bimillennial. Share some ideas on how your group could use the occasion to do something great for your community.

Is there a historical landmark to be preserved? Would a local community service project or art exhibit best express the spirit of the bimillennial? Or would your group prefer to express its bimillennial vision in a local pageant, such as a county fair, holiday parade or historical reenactment?

22. Study *The Star of 2000* as a small group.

Do you belong to a prayer group, Bible study group or Sunday school class? You might suggest this book be used as the focus for its meetings during your next quarter. Each member could be encouraged to read a chapter or two before you meet. When you come together, a relevant theme could be covered through sharing, discussion and prayer. See Appendix A for a discussion guide.

23. Develop "Vision 2000" as a church.

Does your congregation have a big-picture plan for the year 2000? Is your parish asking God how it might become all it was meant to be by the bimillennial?

One great guide that your church can use to develop vision and growth goals for the year 2000 is called, *Vision 2000: Planning for ministry into the next century.*[9] Included are guidelines on how to celebrate your corporate vision each year moving up to the bimillennial. It even helps you plan events for the Easter and Christmas season of 2000! Hundreds of congregations and whole districts have become "Vision 2000" churches.

24. Adopt a people by 2000.

About two years ago I traveled to Tampa, Fla., and got the chance to renew acquaintances with an old friend. Before speaking that evening, I brought up the concept of Jesus' 2,000th birthday with my friend, Nick Panico, who is a pastor.

He responded, "I would like to present the Yanoni people of Brazil to the Lord for His 2,000th birthday."

The Yanoni people, I learned, live along the Amazon and have no church of their own. Nick and his congregation have sent several teams to visit the Yanoni people. I immediately thought of the apostle Paul, whose great ambition was to present whole peoples unto God, sanctified by the Holy Spirit.

There are hundreds of groups like the Yanoni that are waiting to be adopted. You might be the very link which gives them the priceless gift of Jesus by 2000, and they might give you one in return. For information, contact Adopt-A-People, P.O. Box 1795, Colorado Springs, CO 80901, (719) 473-8800.

25. Convene a "celebrate 2000" forum in your city.

If you are a church or ministry leader in your community, you might convene a one-day "celebrate 2000" forum where leaders from various networks can discuss the meaning of the bimillennial and its application for your community.

From 1996 to 2001, bimillennial tributes to Jesus will likely fill our city's churches, theaters, libraries, museums and stadiums. Through a "celebrate 2000" forum, the vision for Jesus' bimillennial can be presented, and leaders of various groups, from congregations and prayer networks to evangelism and community ministries, can interact with one another.

The time frame to plan a successful forum is four to six months. Leaders usually respond when personally invited by other leaders they know and respect. Once they pre-register, this book could be sent out as a briefing document.

If your "celebrate 2000" forum is successful, your convening committee might continue its work as a city-wide bimillennial task force. Its function would not be to sponsor all bimillennial events in your area, but to provide encouragement and coordination as the commemorative pace quickens.

For resources on how-to cultivate a city-wide network among church leaders, contact: Mission America 2000, 901 E. 78th St., Minneapolis, MN 55420-1300, (612) 853-1741.

In the desert prepare a way for the Lord,
make straight . . . a highway for our God.
—Isaiah 40:3

12

Builders for the Third Millennium

In 1991, Olgy and I came to the end of our line. Due to financial pressures, it seemed like our days of serving God were over. Debts had piled up. Owning a home was out of our reach in the Los Angeles real estate market. My consulting work had dried up, and no one was knocking on our door in regards to the bimillennial.

At that time, I noticed the ministry of Jesus had only commenced after He had been tested in the wilderness. I began to pray, "Lord, let this be my appointed time. Prove your call to me, shorten my wilderness experience, and bring us into jubilee." I set aside the month of February to seek the Lord, and fasted more than usual.

About three weeks later, things seemed to break over my life. I had a spiritual dream which gave me great hope that our journey to the Star of 2000 had not ended. Here is what I wrote in my journal the following morning:

> Last night I dreamed I was playing on a basketball team with old high school buddies. Later, we walked to my house. In the back yard I saw a portal open, a shaft of

light, a path extended down from the sky, from the presence of God. I rushed into the back yard, encouraging my friends to join me.

We got on this path which was quite wide, like a four-lane highway. Looking up, we could see it led to Jesus, whose reflection was in the clouds. This began a day and a half journey to God. We were all pilgrims before God, climbing, and resting, then rising the next day and seeking fellowship with Him.

He did not appear in person, but we knew we were very near to Him. Our journey ended at a retreat place, close to the very courts of God. We were shown upstairs rooms where we were to stay that night. The next morning we would have an appointment with God.

I remember coming down to the audience hall, where our appointment was to be the next morning. It was a rectangular living room with a fireplace on one long wall. I sensed if we would come the next morning, He would come to us—at this meeting ground between heaven and earth.

The rest of the dream is sketchy, but I did mention this to others in the neighborhood, that they too could seek God. Never before have I had such intense feelings of joy.

This makes me feel that the house of God is not far away, it is very close. I can't help but feel that revival for my generation may be very real and very near.

This experience confirmed what we had already sensed—that a jubilee season of ministry was about to begin.

Over the next nine months, the Lord enabled us to relocate our family to Colorado Springs, restart our ministry and buy a miracle home.God does have a sense of humor. To remind me of this dream, our home is in the "Skyway" subdivision.

Through the grace of God we have gotten a new lease on life. My wife Olgy tells me she feels ten years younger!

A Highway for God

The ancient Near East had the custom of sending royal heralds ahead to prepare the way for the visit of a monarch. A king would send his herald to a city or country he ruled over to announce his imminent visit. The emphasis was never on the herald, but on the presence of the sovereign, who followed in procession. The prophet Isaiah once heard the voice of a herald shouting:

> In the desert prepare the way for the Lord,
> make straight in the wilderness
> a highway for our God.
> Every valley shall be raised up,
> every mountain and hill made low;
> the rough ground shall become level,
> the rugged places a plain.
> And the glory of the Lord will be revealed,
> and all mankind together will see it
> (Isaiah 40:3-5).

To help celebrate Canada's centennial year in 1967, the French head of state, General Charles de Gaulle, was invited. In preparation, they scrubbed Highway 40, the Trans-Canada Highway, from Quebec City to Montreal, and painted fleur de lys[1] down the center line—all one hundred and fifty miles of it—so that as his cavalcade rolled into Expo, he would feel welcomed.[2]

If a country would go to such a great extent to welcome a visiting head of state, what does that say about our preparations for the bimillennial of Jesus?

As we prepare for A.D. 2000, I believe we need to see our role as heralds and builders of this spiritual highway for God, in anticipation of His visitation. When asked who he was in reference to Christ, John the Baptist answered with the ancient cry of Isaiah, "I am the voice of one calling in the desert, 'Make straight the way for the Lord'" (John 1:23).

The American Bicentennial

I was just finishing high school in 1971 when the United States formally opened it's bicentennial era. Back then we mainly thought about the bicentennial of the American Revolution coming in the summer of '76. Yet twenty years later we were still celebrating the bicentennial! Why? Because the United States had more than one bicentennial. The one in 1976 celebrated the 200th anniversary of the Declaration of Independence. The one in 1987 celebrated the bicentennial of the Constitution.

The realization that mega-anniversaries can often stretch across many years came to me one morning while I was reading the *Los Angeles Times*. On December 6, 1991 I turned the page to find a half-page ad for the "Bill of Rights" on wheels. It was coming to schools and malls in our area. Underneath the graphic of the van were these words:

Bill of Rights
BICENTENNIAL
1791–1991

A right perspective of the American bicentennial era would recognize its opening in 1971, and its conclusion in 1991, with a celebration of the Bill of Rights. In between would be the two major bicentennials, Independence Day in 1976, and the Constitution in 1987.

The Two Bimillennials

What does this have to do with the 2,000th anniversary of the birth of Jesus?

Namely this: if it took us 20 years to celebrate the American bicentennial, it may take us 40 years to celebrate our world's bimillennial.

The Spirit of God may well be orchestrating such events that we will look back in 40 years and say that in 1996 we entered the bimillennial era. Next, in the year 2000, we celebrated the first bimillennial: Jesus' 2,000th birthday. Then, in the year 2033, if our Lord tarries, we celebrated the *second* bimillennial: the 2,000th anniversary of Christ's triumph over death and the birth of His church.

We might call this the bimillennial epoch, a 40-year period of time in which these two bimillennials of Christ are recognized, understood and commemorated.

The first bimillennial in 2000 will likely define the opening hour of the new millennium. The second in 2033 will define the opening half of the 21st century. Taken together, these two bimillennials will be like a paved airport strip, a runway for the third Christian millennium.

A Thousand Year Conspiracy

We must not take the advent of the third millennium for granted. With unbridled brutality and bloodletting, Hitler's Third Reich conspired to steal the next millennium. The Nazi propaganda apparatus staged grandiose rituals and huge party rallies. An account of the Nuremberg rally in 1936 describes a crowd of 140,000 people at night witnessing 25,000 flag-bearers solemnly marching out of the darkness into floodlight. A mass choir then sung patriotic songs to set the stage for Hitler.

Today, scholars are realizing that fascism was essentially a spiritual movement, in revolt against the Judeo-Christian idea of God and transcendent moral laws. At its core, fascism sought to exalt the nation-state, disregard the individual and smash the monuments of Western civilization.[3]

Hitler declared his Third Reich would last for a millennium. He set out to steal the next 1,000 years of history—but God smashed him.

It's ironic that the 20th century produced such a madman with a focused vision for the third millennium, while we in society, have hardly considered what it means. No one knows all what the third millennium might bring. One thing we do know for sure is that the later ages of history will witness a greater reign and rule of Christ.

The Quest for the Unknown

In 1985 two British futurists wrote a book entitled *The Third Millennium*.[4] In essence, it is a history of times to come. Cast in the form of a narrative written in the year 3000 A.D., the book looks back on the third millennium through such topics as:

- the period of crisis, 2000 to 2180
- the period of recovery, 2180 to 2400
- the period of transformation, 2400 to 2650
- the creation of the new world, 2650 to 3000.

And what epochs they were! Here events unfolded such as:

- the last nuclear war in 2079 between Argentina and Brazil, resulting in a worldwide permanent ban on nuclear weapons.
- the global warming crisis of 2015, in which seas rose and floods hit coastal cities.
- the greening of the moon and other outer space places in the 25th century.
- the controversial high space mining of asteroid belts through fusion bombs.
- the genetic engineering of human merpeople and underwater colonies.

No one can say whether we will make it to the year 3000, but I was thrilled to read the quest for the unknown was still alive at the trimillennial of Christ.

As the authors write, "The horizons of the human enterprise now stretch to infinity, but that does not mean we can see all that lies within them."

As we reach the year 2000, may we renew our common quest for the greater truth of the mystery of the one and true God, whose power, majesty and glory will be fully unveiled at the end of time.

Our Journey Toward Hope

I see the star of 2000 rising as a new day dawns. If you look carefully in the heavens, you can see it too. This stellar year beckons us to embark on a journey toward hope. It calls us to discover Christ anew and invite the world to sing with us, "Oh, come let us adore Him."

The bimillennial calls us to come before the King, and to come under a reign which began two thousand years ago when the angels sang,

> "Glory to God in the highest,
> and on earth peace, good will to men."

Our journey as Magi must not stop there. Adoration and worship must prepare the way for consecration and service. If the bimillennial of Christ is to have any hope of more than a passing success, it must give birth to "a spirit of 2000" which can bring renewal and awakening to all walks of life at the dawn of the third millennium.

When you wish upon a star,
your dream comes true.

A Prayer of the
Fourth Wise Man

On the eve of the bimillennial, Zalshar, the fourth wise man, found himself gazing more each night into the heavens.

Then one evening, it suddenly appeared. Morning was just about to break when Jupiter and Saturn strolled together like two saffron flames merging into one.

As Zalshar watched, a royal blue spark burst out of the darkness beneath. Jupiter emerged wearing a magnificent mantle of light.

"This is the heavenly sign," Zalshar cried. "The morning Star is soon to arise in every heart. Another journey of the Magi must surely begin." Before embarking, Zalshar lifted up his eyes to heaven and prayed,

> Oh sovereign Lord,
> Father of lights,
> hear the prayer of your servant
> on this cold starry night.
>
> My journey has taken me
> across many lands,

on horses and camels
to seek the Son of Man.

Through the centuries
I have wandered in search of thy Star,
looking for the true spirit of giving,
both near and far.

As the church lifts her eyes to
see the star of your Son,
give her a spirit of wisdom
that they all might be one.

Let her bring forth gifts of adoration
like my brother Magi of long ago,
treasures of pure devotion
so the world will clearly know.

Oh sovereign Lord,
the fullness of time is at hand,
Glorify your Son in your presence
with the glory He had when the world began.

When I consider the heavens,
the awesome work of your hands,
Let a temple to Christ be built
so a new memorial might stand.

Send forth your holy angels
from the East to the West,
to gather praises and tributes
to present to Christ our best.

As this happens in heaven,
On earth may awakening come.
As we celebrate the greatest Christmas ever
May your will be done.

                                    Amen.

Endnotes

Prologue: A Parable of the Fourth Wise Man

1. The only mention of the Magi in Scripture comes from Matthew 2:1-16. The traditional number of three wise men has been inferred from the three gifts mentioned: gold, frankincense and myrrh. All the rest, including the names of Gaspar, Melchoir and Balthasar, derive from early apocryphal writings and stories written in the Middle Ages.

The legend of a fourth king who started farther away than the others, missed the nativity in Bethlehem and wandered until Good Friday, has been told by Henry Van Dyke (1852-1933), in his 1895 classic, *The Story of the Other Wise Man.*

The parable in this prologue is my creation, inspired in part by Jim Bradford's nativity play, "Journey to the Light." Our journey toward 2000 is much like the journey of the original Magi. I trust my parable of Zalshar, while fictional, reminds us we are all Magi at heart if we come into His presence and adore Him.

2. The star of Bethlehem is only mentioned in the Gospel of Matthew (Matthew 2:2,7,9-10). Little did he know he would keep

astronomers and historians busy for 2,000 years speculating on
its nature! The various theories about the "star" all have early
origins: it was a comet (c. A.D. 248), it was a planetary con-
junction of Jupiter and Saturn (c. A.D. 800), or it was a nova
(1729). All three heavenly phenomena were observed in the period
from 7 to 5 B.C., the best estimate for the birth of Christ.

The uncertainty in the date of Christ's birth and the rather
general descriptions of astronomical phenomena of that day,
leaves open many possibilities for astronomical explanations
of the star of Bethlehem.

Curiously enough, Jupiter was struck by a comet in July of
1994, leading some people to compare this phenomena to the
star of Bethlehem.

3. The real "Star" which is rising as we approach the year
2000 is Jesus. When the word "Star" is capitalized in this book,
it refers to Him. Christ is the true light of the world, the real
Star and celebrity of the year 2000. Our journey of hope leads
to Him. For Scriptural references to Christ as the morning Star,
see Numbers 24:17, 2 Peter 2:19 and Revelation 22:16.

Chapter 1: The Bimillennial Era Has Begun

1. Gary, Jay and Olgy, eds. *The Countdown Has Begun: The
story of the global consultation on AD 2000*, AD 2000 Global
Service Office, 1989.

Chapter 2: Unwrap History's Mystery

1. Cited by Mead, Frank. *The Encyclopedia of Religious
Quotations*, Revell, 1965, p. 57.

2. Pelikan, Jaroslav. *Jesus Through the Centuries: His place
in the history of culture*, Harper & Row, 1987, p. 1.

3. Bright, Bill. *A Man Without Equal*, New Life Publications, 1991, p. 12-13.

4. "The Originality of Jesus" by George A. Gordon, in *The
Story of Jesus in the World's Literature*, edited by Edward
Wagenknecht. Creative Age Press, 1946, p. 240-241.

5. "The Incomparable Christ." Oradell, N.J.: American Tract Society, n.d.

6. As quoted in: Schaff, Philip. *The Person of Christ*, George H. Doran Company, 1913, p. 137, 138.

7. Küng, Hans. *On Being a Christian*, english translation, Doubleday, 1976, p. 145.

8. Cited by Frank Mead, *The Encyclopedia of Religious Quotations*, Revell, 1965, p. 49.

9. Ghandi, Mahatma. *What Jesus Means to Me*, compiled by P.K. Prabhu, Navajivan Publishing House, 1959, p. 9.

10. Donovan, Vincent. *The Church in the Midst of Creation*, Orbis Books, 1989, p. 51.

Chapter 3: Something Beautiful for God
1. Winter, Ralph. "The Challenge of the Year 2000," Pasadena, Calif., address given May 27, 1982.

2. The first book to document the remarkable spread of A.D. 2000 plans within the Christian movement was: Barrett, David B. and James W. Reapsome, *Seven Hundred Plans to Evangelize the World: The rise of a global movement*, New Hope, 1988.

3. Vischer, Lukas. "A Holy Year?" Midstream: An Ecumenical Journal, October, 1987, p. 513.

Chapter 4: The Reason for the Season
1. Johnston, William M. *Celebrations: The cult of anniversaries in Europe and the United States today*, Transaction Publishers, 1991.

2. Correspondence from the author, February 24, 1993. Used by permission.

3. Durant, Will. *Caesar and Christ*, Simon and Schuster, 1944, p. 557.

4. Quoted in Hunter, James Davidson and Guinness, Os, eds., *Articles of Faith, Articles of Peace*, The Brookings Institution, 1990, p. v.

5. Howard Thurman, "The Work of Christmas," *The Mood of Christmas*, Friends University Press, 1973.

6. One way to link each year of the bimillennial era to some aspect of Jesus' life and legacy might be as follows:

1996: Jesus—Herald of Jubilee
1997: Jesus—King of Kings
1998: Jesus—Prince of Peace
1999: Jesus—Hope of History
2000: Jesus—Source of Civilization
2001: Jesus—Lord of the Universe

7. Stewart, Ed. *Millennium's Eve*, Victor, 1993.

Chapter 5: A Powerful Mega-Image

1. Hartje, Robert G. *Bicentennial USA: Pathways to celebration*, AASLH, 1973, p. xiv.

2. The word millennium comes from the Latin word *mille*, meaning "1,000 years, or the 1,000 year reign of Christ." Not to be confused with millennial or bimillennial, which refer to the anniversary of an event that occurred 1,000 or 2,000 years ago.

3. Naisbitt, John and Patricia Aburdene. *Megatrends 2000: Ten new directions for the 1990's*, William Morrow, 1990, p. 11-17, 295-297.

4. Asimov, Isaac and Frank White. *The March of the Millennia: A key to looking at history*. Walker, 1991, p. 183.

5. A good book in this category is Tom Sine's *Wild Hope: Living with confidence in the face of future shock*, Word, 1991.

6. Naisbitt and Aburdene. *Megatrends 2000*, p. 17.

7. Sitarz, Daniel, ed., *Agenda 21: The earth summit strategy to save our planet*, EarthPress, 1993.

8. *AD 2000 Global Monitor*, P.O. Box 129, Rockville, VA 23146.

9. Barrett, David and James Reapsome. *Our Globe and How to Reach It: A manual for the decade of evangelism*, New Hope, 1990.

10. Kuzmic, Peter, "How to Teach the Truth of the Gospel," in *Proclaim Christ Until He Comes*, J.D. Douglas, ed., World Wide Publications, 1990, p. 200.

11. In and of themselves, the four mega-images introduced up to this point have helped us look to the year 2000, but have yet to integrate the bimillennial of Jesus into their approach. This will likely change as we move into the last half of the '90s.

Chapter 6: We are the Jubilee Generation

1. Ringe, Sharon. *Jesus, Liberation, and the Biblical Jubilee: Images for ethics and Christology*, Fortress Press, 1985, p. 7-10.

2. Schwartz, Hillel. *Century's End: A cultural history of the fin de siècle from the 990s through the 1990s*, Doubleday, 1990, p. 58.

3. Colson, Charles. "The Enduring Revolution: 1993 Templeton Address," Prison Fellowship, Washington, DC, 20041–0500, p. 12-14.

4. Campolo, Tony. *The Kingdom of God is a Party: God's radical plan for His family*, Word, 1990, p. 25-27.

Chapter 7: The Anniversary Attraction

1. In looking for hints as to what the year 2000 might bring, many have looked at the year 1000 for clues. Rather than festivity, the year 1000 called forth fear—or so we are led to believe. But the "legend of the year 1000" is just that—a legend. According to the last hundred years of scholarship, the "panic terror" across Europe in 999 never happened (Schwartz, *Century's End*, p. 3-8).

The legend of the year 1000 was largely a creation by 18th century writers who wished to portray the church as superstitious. Ironically, modern men, not medieval believers, seem to be the ones infected with "millennial madness."

2. Collins, Gail and Dan. *The Millennium Book: Your essential all-purpose guide for the year 2000*, Doubleday, 1991.

3. Muller, Robert. *The First Lady of the World*, World Happiness and Cooperation, 1991, p. 196-197.

4. Dawson, John. *Taking our Cities for God: How to break spiritual strongholds*, Creation House, 1989.

5. Aykroyd, Peter. *The Anniversary Compulsion: Canada's centennial celebrations—a model mega-anniversary*, Dundurn Press, 1992, p. 11.

Chapter 8: A Symphony of Praise
1. Swimme, Brian and Thomas Berry. *The Universe Story: A celebration of the unfolding of the cosmos*, Harper Collins, 1992, p. 263-264.

2. Bryant, David. *The Hope at Hand: The world revival for the 21st Century*, Baker Books, 1995.

Chapter 9: The March of the Millennium
1. McCullough, Colleen. *A Creed for the Third Millennium*, Harper & Row, 1985.

2. I am indebted to Steve Hawthorne for these insights. He points to five major processions in the Scriptures, each which ended at the house of God.

3. In order to see the larger canvas of tribute and honor being brought unto Christ, we need to recover a "theology of glory." We need to see how humanity receives "the glory of the Lord" such that it might be given to God in Jesus Christ. For the theologically inclined, I recommend Hans Urs Von Balthasar's seven volume series, *The Glory of the Lord: A theological aesthetics*, Ignatius Press, 1982.

4. "Let the Flame Burn Brighter," adm. in the U.S.A. by Integrity's Hosanna! Music, Mobile, AL. All rights reserved.

5. Kendrick, Graham. *Public Praise: Celebrating Jesus on the streets of the world*, Creation House, 1992.

Chapter 10: The Celebration of Civilization
1. Toynbee, Arnold. *Civilization on Trial*, Oxford University Press, 1948, p. 5.

2. Kennedy, Paul. *Preparing for the Twenty-First Century*, Random House, 1993, p. 334.

3. Donovan, Vincent. *Christianity Rediscovered*, Orbis Books, 1978, p. 184.

Chapter 11: Light Two Thousand Candles

1. Colson, Chuck. Foreword to *You Can Be a Point of Light* by Loux, Gordon and Ronald E. Wilson, Multnomah, 1991, p. 9-11.

2. Hurlburt, C.E. and T.C. Horton. *The Wonderful Names of Our Wonderful Lord*, Barbour & Co., n.d..

3. *His Face: Images of Christ in art*, Chameleon Books, 1988.

4. Keeley, Robin, ed. *Jesus 2000: A major investigation into history's most intriguing figure*, Lion, 1989.

5. L'Engle, Madeleine. *The Irrational Season*, Harper, 1977.

6. Ade Scofield, Tiffany and John Moore Hines. *Dull Dinners into Sacred Feasts: A guide to household celebrations of the church year*, St. Andrew's Episcopal Church, Louisville, KY, 40205.

7. Mains, Karen. *Making Sunday Special*, Word, 1987.

8. Adler, Mortimer J. and William Gorman, eds. *The Great Ideas: A syntopicon of great books of the Western world*, Encyclopedia Britannica, 1952.

9. Harding, Joe and Ralph Mohney. *Vision 2000: Planning for ministry into the next century*, Discipleship Resources, 1991.

Chapter 12: Builders for the Third Millennium

1. The *fleur de lys* is one of the world's most readily recognizable symbols of royalty. Named after France's Louis VII, the "flower of Louis" became the official emblem of French royalty.

2. Aykroyd, Peter. *The Anniversary Compulsion*, Dundurn Press, 1992, p. 117.

3. Veith, Jr., Gene Edward. *Modern Fascism: Liquidating the Judeo-Christian worldview*, Concordia, 1993.

4. Stableford, Brian and David Langford. *The Third Millennium: A history of the world, AD 2000–3000*, Knopf, 1985.

Discussion Guide

This appendix contains *The Star of 2000* discussion guide for personal and small group reflection.

Chapter 1: The Bimillennial Era Has Begun
1. How is our journey to the bimillennial like the journey of the Magi?
2. How are people getting ready to celebrate the 2,000th anniversary of the birth of Jesus?
3. How is the bimillennial era defined? What might characterize it?
4. How is our approach to A.D. 2000 changing as we move through this decade?
5. Prior to this study, what did you think about the year 2000?

Chapter 2: Unwrap History's Mystery
1. In comparison to others in history, in what ways do you consider Jesus to be unique?
2. What do you consider to be Jesus' greatest gifts to world civilization?

3. What have other world leaders seen in Jesus?
4. Read Colossians 1:15-20, 25-27. How does Paul describe Christ? In what ways are His "unsearchable riches" still a mystery?
5. What would it look like for the world to experience "a God-given awakening of interest in the person of Jesus as we move toward 2000"?

Chapter 3: Something Beautiful for God
1. How did Mary of Bethany give Jesus her greatest gift?
2. What characteristics do you see in Mary of Bethany that you would like to emulate?
3. What might be your greatest gift to Christ as we approach His 2,000th anniversary?
4. What are some of the key milestones in the development of the bimillennial from the mid–'70s until now.

Chapter 4: The Reason for the Season
1. What activities and events might characterize the "greatest Christmas ever"?
2. What reason did the academic scholar have for not mentioning Jesus' bimillennial in his book? Was it valid?
3. What lessons does Columbus' quincentennial teach us in reference to Jesus' bimillennial?
4. In what way might the celebrations of Jesus' bimillennial develop beyond a Christmas year theme?

Chapter 5: A Powerful Mega-Image
1. In what way was this chapter helpful in your understanding of A.D. 2000?
2. What is an A.D. 2000 mega-image?
3. In your own words, describe the four different approaches to the bimillennial over the past 30 years.
4. In reference to defining Jesus' bimillennial, what are the strengths and weaknesses of each of these mega-images?

Chapter 6: We Are the Jubilee Generation

1. What things are replaced and what things are restored in a Year of Jubilee according to Leviticus 25, Isaiah 61:1-4 or Luke 4:18-19?
2. Why do we say that Jesus has inaugurated a perpetual jubilee?
3. Why does the author feel the Jubilee year of 2000 could not have come at a better time?
4. What inheritance have we lost as a modern society?
5. How does true celebration differ from mere partying?

Chapter 7: The Anniversary Attraction

1. How is the world preparing to celebrate the year 2000?
2. Why will the year 2000 bring such a mixture of secular and sacred celebrations?
3. What is "spiritual procession"? How does that compare and contrast with "spiritual warfare"?
4. In your own words, describe the three preparatory steps to spiritual procession?
5. In what way do you feel led to prepare your city for Jesus' bimillennial?

Chapter 8: A Symphony of Praise

1. Read Psalm 148. In what way could this Psalm be considered a hymn of the universe?
2. What did the "chop sticks" story mean to you personally?
3. How do the Concert of Prayer distinctives focus our prayers for A.D. 2000?
4. Why is a biblical vision of the house of God so foundational to the bimillennial?
5. In what ways have you experienced a rebirth of worship in your life? In what ways would you like to experience it as you prepare for the bimillennial?

Chapter 9: The March of the Millennium

1. In what way have public marches defined our century, for good or bad?
2. In what way is Jesus leading a greater "March of the Millennium?" Cite biblical passages to support your answer.
3. What should the concepts of "tribute, honor and glory" mean to us?
4. Have you ever participated in a "March for Jesus"? If so, what did it mean to you?

Chapter 10: The Celebration of Civilization

1. Describe the "unfinished task" in spiritual and economic terms? What does this have to do with the cradle of civilization?
2. How does speaking in terms of "unbegun relationships" expand our horizons beyond that of the "unfinished task"?
3. In what way, if any, do you identify with Sandi?
4. From a biblical and cultural point of view, what is the celebration of civilization?
5. What personal steps could we take as a family or a group to insure that the bimillennial is truly an international and intercultural celebration?

Chapter 11: Light Two Thousand Candles

1. What inspired you as you read Andy Lakey's story?
2. How do you intend to light a candle for Christ in honor of His 2000th birthday:

    —in your heart?

    —in your home?

    —in your community?

3. In what way do you see yourself spreading the vision for Jesus' celebration 2000?

Chapter 12: Builders for the Third Millennium

1. What is the most memorable dream you have had? What spiritual lesson, if any, did it teach you?
2. Describe the role of one who builds a spiritual highway for God?
3. In what way can the two American bicentennials be compared to Christs' two bimillennials?
4. What does the advent of the third millennium mean to you? What ought it mean to society?
5. To the careful reader, *The Star of 2000* revealed ten mega-trends, or new directions the second half of the '90s will likely witness. Which shift in thinking has meant the most to you? Why?

    —Calendar of 2000 → Christ of 2000

    —Decade of Harvest → Celebration of Centuries

    —Jesus of History → Christ as an Unveiled Mystery

    —Biggest New Year's Ever → Greatest Christmas Ever

    —Milestone of 2000 → Mega-Anniversary of 2000

    —Terminal Generation → Jubilee Generation

    —Taking Our Cities For God → Taking Our Cities To God

    —Spiritual Warfare → Spiritual Procession

    —Unfinished Task → Unbegun Relationships

    —Century's End → Advent of Third Millennium

6. What is your prayer on the eve of the bimillennial?

Bibliography

This appendix offers selective reading for further celebration 2000 study. Many of these books are available through: Bimillennial Press, P.O. Box 1777, Colorado Springs, CO 80901. Write for a catalogue.

Allison, Lora. *Celebration: Banners, dance and holiness in worship.* Sonrise, 1987.

Aykroyd, Peter H. *The Anniversary Compulsion: Canada's centennial celebrations, a model mega-anniversary.* Dundurn, 1992.

Bellamy, Edward. *Looking Backward: 2000–1887.* Harvard, 1967 (1888).

Bryant, David. *The Hope at Hand: World revival for the 21st century.* Baker, 1995.

Campolo, Tony. *The Kingdom of God is a Party: God's radical plan for his family.* Word, 1990.

Collins, Gail and Dan. *The Millennium Book: Your essential all-purpose guide for the year 2000*. Doubleday, 1991.

Gary, Jay. *The Star of 2000: Our journey toward hope*. Bimillennial Press, 1994.

Gary, Jay and Olgy. *The Countdown Has Begun: The story of the global consultation on AD 2000*. AD 2000 Global Service Office, 1989.

Guinness, Os. *The American Hour: A time of reckoning and the once and future role of faith*. Free Press, 1993.

Harding, Joe and Ralph Mohney. *Vision 2000: Planning for ministry into the next century*. Discipleship Resources, 1991.

Hartje, Robert G. *Bicentennial USA: Pathways to celebration*. American Association of State and Local Historians, 1973.

Johnston, William M. *Celebrations: The cult of anniversaries in Europe and the United States today*. Transaction, 1991.

Kendrick, Graham. *Public Praise: Celebrating Jesus on the streets of the world*. Creation House, 1992.

Manning, Frank E., ed. *The Celebration of Society: Perspectives on contemporary cultural performance*. Bowling Green, 1983.

Pelikan, Jaroslav. *Jesus Through the Centuries: His place in the history of culture*. Harper & Row, 1985.

Petersen, Keith. *Historical Celebrations: A handbook for organizers of diamond jubilees, centennials, and other community anniversaries*. Idaho State Historical Society, 1986.

Schwartz, Hillel. *Century's End: A cultural history of the fin de siècle from the 990s through the 1990s*. Doubleday, 1990.

Thurston, Herbert. *The Holy Year of Jubilee: An account of the history and ceremonial of the Roman Jubilee*. Sands, 1900.

Resource Directory

This appendix recommends bimillennial magazines, training, tours and tapes.

Action Music
P.O. Box 2802, Freemont, CA 94536, (510) 487-8533. Offers music cassettes on the year 2000.

AD 2000 & Beyond Movement
2860 S. Circle Dr., Suite 2112, Colorado Springs, CO 80906, (719) 576-2000. Offers conferences on A.D. 2000.

Angel Gallery
3257 S.E. Hawthorne Blvd., Portland, OR 97214, (503) 239-5330. Offers commemorative Angel 2000 pins and paintings by Andy Lakey.

Celebration 2000
P.O. Box 1777, Colorado Springs, CO 80901, (719) 636-2000. Provides bimillennial newsletters, books, speakers and networking opportunities.

Club 2000

6060 Fenton, Suite 8, Dept. C, Livermore, CA 94550, (510) 449-3284. Creates unique year 2000 products for resale.

Concerts of Prayer International

P.O. Box 1399, Wheaton, IL 60189, (708) 690-8441. Resources to organize a prayer concert in your city.

Global Harvest Ministries

215 N. Marengo St., #151, Pasadena, CA 91001, (818) 577-7122. Distributes an AD 2000 *Prayer Track* newsletter for evangelicals.

International Worship Leaders' Institute

P.O. Box 130, Bedford, TX 76095, (817) 540-1826. Offers national and regional training schools on how to lead worship.

Jesus 2000

P.O. Box 2510, Chattanooga, TN 37409, (615) 821-3635. Offers commemorative congresses and tours of Israel.

March for Jesus-U.S.A.

P.O. Box 3216, Austin, TX 78764, (512) 416-0066. Resources to organize a praise march in your city.

Mission America 2000

901 E. 78th St., Minneapolis, MN 55420-1300, (612) 853-1741. Resources for city-wide strategy among churches for 2000.

New Evangelization 2000

P.O. Box 479, Lincroft, NJ 07738–0479, (908) 530-3446. Distributes an A.D. 2000 magazine for Catholics.

New Life 2000

100 Sunport Lane, Orlando, FL 32809, (407) 826-2000. Offers local & international programs which feature the use of the *JESUS* film or video for a community.

Glossary

A.D.—abbreviation for *Anno Domini* (Latin), "the Year of Our Lord;" in reference to the count of years measured from the birth of Christ, arbitrarily fixed as A.D. 1. Properly, A.D. should precede references to a specific year, such as A.D. 2000. When neither B.C. nor A.D. accompanies a date, it is usually understood that the year is part of our present calendar. Dating by A.D. was adopted in 525.

B.C.—Abbreviation for "Before Christ," as in 44 B.C. This notation of counting backwards from the birth of Christ first appeared in the seventeenth century.

Bimillennial—an anniversary or celebration of an event that occurred 2,000 years earlier, such as the 2,000th anniversary of the birth of Jesus.

Bimillennial era—a period of years which commemorate a 2,000-year anniversary, with steps of recognition, preparation and observation. The bimillennial era of Jesus will likely unfold from 1996 to 2001.

Bimillennium—a 2,000-year period or celebrations relating to that epoch of history.

C.E.—abbreviation for Common Era. A secular reference used in place of A.D., meant to function without reference to the Christian Era or birth of Christ. Used to precede references to specific years, such as C.E. 1984. B.C.E. means "Before the Common Era," as in 44 B.C.E. The common civil calendar was universally adopted in this century.

Jubilee—the celebration of special anniversaries, or occasions such as the 50th (golden jubilee). In Hebrew law it was a year of celebration observed by Jews once every 50 years, in modern Roman Catholic law, every 25 years.

Mega-anniversary—a great anniversary of significant magnitude, like a centennial, quincentennial, millennial, bimillennial or trimillennial of a notable event, such as the birth of a founder of a religion, nation or civilization.

Mega-image—a mental conception, paradigm or framework used to envision the future. Five A.D. 2000 mega-images have shaped our approach to the year 2000.

Redemptive gift—a notable capacity, endowment or collective talent which operates to bring peace, justice and righteousness to the life of a city.

Spiritual procession—the act of moving into the presence of God; a series of celebratory events, whether praise marches, prayer rallies, worship symposiums or drama festivals which aim to take a city to God.

Third millennium—the coming period of history, A.D. 2000–3000, which technically begins January 1, 2001, signifying our entry into the third Christian millennium.

Year 2000—a time with both religious and cultural meaning. The year 2000 is both 1) the 2,000th anniversary of the birth of Christ, and 2) the bimillennium of our universal civil calendar.

Index

About the Author

JAY GARY has been writing and speaking on the year 2000 for more than a decade.

Jay is the director of Celebration 2000—a consulting group formed in 1989 to support creative projects whose aim is to commemorate the 2,000th anniversary of the birth of Christ.

He is the author of *The Countdown Has Begun* which shares how leaders are joining hands to touch the world for Christ by the year 2000.

From 1986 to 1989, Jay served as a conference planner with the Lausanne movement, a network launched by Billy Graham. From 1976 to 1986, Jay worked as a pastor to college students, a mission educator and a magazine editor.

Jay and his wife, Olgy, have been married since 1978 and have two children, David and Christine. They reside in Colorado Springs, Colo.

For additional information on the issues raised in this book, write the author at: Celebration 2000, P.O. Box 1777, Colorado Springs, CO 80901-1777.

Follow the Star of 2000

Nothing encourages us more than to hear how someone has seen the Star of 2000 and begun a journey toward hope. With your permission, we would like to share your experience with others through our newsletter or in future books. Write us at the address below.

For more information regarding "The Star of 2000" project, including articles, research, newsletters, tapes, seminars and keynote addresses, please call (719) 636-2000 or write to: Celebration 2000, P.O. Box 1777, Colorado Springs, CO 80901-1777.